LIFE

IN THE

GOAT LANE

For Martha & Woody,
great friends & great
people.
            Best always,
                Linda Fink

LIFE IN THE GOAT LANE

Tales From *The Kidding Pen*

by

Linda Fink

Illustrations by Barbara Millikan

Rickreall Creek House • Oregon

Printed in the United States of America on recycled, acid-free paper

Published by Rickreall Creek House, Box 13, Rickreall, Oregon 97371

ISBN 0-943149-09-6

Library of Congress Catalog Card Number 90-62907

For my husband, Johnny,
chief fence and barn builder, relief milker,
and my best friend...
even though he thinks I have too many goats.

ACKNOWLEDGMENTS

Many thanks to Kim Pease, publisher of *United Caprine News*, for believing in me back in 1983 and publishing my humor column, "The Kidding Pen", every month since. The chapters in this book are adapted from those Kidding Pen columns. Also thanks to Sue Henry for editing and advising; Barbara Millikan for her wonderful drawings and the title; my son Steve Fink for editing, formatting, and computer taming; my son Kevin Fink for formatting and computer taming (without my sons I would have thrown the cantankerous computer behind the sofa and gone back to my old manual typewriter); and everyone who has applauded, prodded and kept me going, including Jerry Easterling, Lee Crawley Kirk, and, especially, Johnny Fink. Also thanks to those of you who bought this book. To those who are thinking about buying it, please do. I need money for goat feed.

PREFACE

Some people live life in the fast lane. I live life in the goat lane. A lane that is, according to my husband, full of crazy drivers. Johnny thinks "goat people" are a little odd.

The goat project started out rationally enough. We both wanted a home milk supply. And I wanted a home milk supply that wouldn't permanently disable me if it stepped on my feet. So we bought a goat.

Angel quickly taught us that goats come in pairs, at the very least. They like company. They *insist* on company. We either had to buy a companion for Angel, or resign ourselves to having a goat in the house, dancing on the dining room table and sleeping in bed -- between us. So we bought Merry.

From those first two flop-eared Nubians, things escalated, as things do with goats. Take one doe, breed her to a buck, and five months later you have milk... and more goats. Cute little kid goats that you can't bear to part with. Soon our two goats had become thirty.

By then, we had acquired our own buck and learned why goats have the reputation for smelling bad. Angel and Merry had no odor at all. Does don't. Bucks are a different story. The buck's musk glands are designed to attract every doe within fifty miles and repel everything else. And they do.

We also learned that some people (like me) get very attached to goats, and tend to spend all their time either with their animals or talking about them. Others (like Johnny) prefer a normal existence. Goat lovers are almost invariably married to goat resisters.

In a very few years, I progressed (or regressed, depending on your point of view) from mere goatkeeper status to that of full-fledged Dairy Goat Breeder. A Dairy Goat Breeder is someone who has too many goats producing too much milk who deliberately breeds them together to create even more goats each producing even more milk. This is called genetic progress. The goat owner progresses from mere eccentricity to udder lunacy.

Then came the show bug. The show bug is an insidious insect that affects livestock breeders the world over. It causes them to spend many hours of hard work and much money dragging their animals around a dusty show ring while slightly saner people watch. I was bitten years ago. There is no cure.

For me and other goat crazies, life in the goat lane revolves around a four season calendar. Here in western Oregon, those seasons tend to run together: kidding season (winter and spring), show season (spring, summer and fall), breeding season (fall and winter), and the-two-weeks-between-the-end-of-breeding-season-and-the-beginning-of-kidding-season.

That is, if we're lucky we have two weeks between the end of breeding season and the beginning of kidding season. That's when we reacquaint ourselves with our families. Sometimes, we're surprised to learn our families have grown up and left home while we were out in the barn trimming hooves.

Life in the Goat Lane is a collection of tales about my twenty, crazy, fun-filled years with goats. The first twenty.

TABLE OF CONTENTS

SHOW SEASON

BREEDING SEASON

THE-TWO-WEEKS-BETWEEN-THE-END-OF-BREEDING-SEASON-AND-THE-BEGINNING-OF-KIDDING-SEASON

KIDDING SEASON

SHOW SEASON

THE ODD COUPLE

Marriages, I've heard, are built on mutual interests. Johnny and I have quite different interests, yet our marriage has lasted nearly twenty-five years. I like raising goats, lots of them. Johnny doesn't. He loves to build things. My building skills are nonexistent. I do emergency repairs only -- six bent nails plus one board and a snarl of baling twine equals one temporarily fixed hole in the fence.

"But look how well those interests complement each other," exclaimed a friend, when I commented on the situation.

"Huh?" I asked.

"You like to raise goats. He likes to build barns and pens."

"Say, you're right! I never thought of it that way!"

Neither had Johnny. When I mentioned my friend's brilliant observation, he snorted.

But it's true, you know. Expanding goat and sheep populations, plus disintegrating fences and buildings, mean Johnny always has some project to keep him occupied. I love the sound of hammer on nail as my dear spouse builds yet another extension on the barn.

What would Johnny do with himself if I didn't give him such wonderful excuses to build things? He'd spend more time away from home, building for other people, that's what. And he loves staying home, working on the farm. Why, I'm just keeping all these animals for HIS sake. I'm sure glad my friend helped me see things so realistically. Here I've been feeling guilty all these years, when I should have been patting myself on the back.

Not every goat lover's spouse is a carpenter who loves to build things, of course. But I'll bet quite a few of them enjoy making money. And if one person wants to make money, surely that person's mate has a duty to spend it. I know one woman who has a fascinating job (to her) and makes gobs of money. Fortunately, her husband is a goat breeder, so she has a place to put all that dough. Else, she wouldn't have an excuse to earn it, would she?

Yes, sir, I think goat owners all over America have been selling themselves short. Here we are, apologizing for our goats, when all this time we've been helping our marriages and the economy. I know my local feed store hopes I never quit raising goats -- half their business comes from me. And the lumber store settles more securely on its financial foundations whenever my husband drives up.

And now I realize that our marriage is stronger for our diversified interests. I used to envy those couples who were both involved in the goat operation, but no longer. What conflicts that must create.

"I want to stay home with the goats. YOU go to work."

"Forget it. I hate my job. I'd rather trim feet and clean pens. YOU go to work."

Thank heavens Johnny doesn't want to do the milking. I love my twice a day ritual in the barn, my head against a soft, warm side; hands rhythmically unleashing that beautiful, fresh, white milk. And what fights we'd have if Johnny wanted a say on which doe should be bred to which buck! Or how the feet should be trimmed. Or, worst of all, how to show a goat.

Many times I've heard a "goat couple" arguing over each other's showmanship abilities, or lack thereof. I can just imagine the fights Johnny and I would have.

"She would have placed higher if you hadn't let her chine dip," I'd berate him in disgust.

"What's a chine dip, something you have with potato chips?"

"No, dummy. That means you let her back sway. The chine is right behind the withers."

"Yeah, she does look kind of withered. Why did you bring her to the show? By the way, the goat you were showing didn't look so great, either. You had her stretched so far she looked like a piece of leather."

Fortunately, Johnny and I never have these arguments. He doesn't come to the shows. That's why our marriage survives. I wouldn't give us five minutes if Johnny wanted to lead a goat into the ring. I don't even like the way he leads them to the van to load.

"Don't strangle her! She's a grand champion!"

"I'm not strangling her, but I will if she doesn't quit dragging me. Why don't you *train* these goats?"

Such minor skirmishes quickly end when the goats are loaded and I've driven out the driveway. Whatever the does do in the show ring is my fault. Johnny is always home ready to congratulate or commiserate when I return.

Goodness yes, having a non-goat lover spouse is a blessing. I never realized it before. And Johnny never realized how lucky he is to have a goat-loving wife who forever needs more pens, more fences, and more barns for him to build. He still doesn't. I asked.

DIESEL-POWERED
CLIPPERS

Dull, rusty electric clipper blades are guaranteed to bring on panic one week before the first show. I should know. I go through it every year. Judges like to *see* the animals they're evaluating, which is difficult when the animal is covered with long, thick, winter hair.

When I clip tails and udders before my does kid, I remind myself to do something about the blades. But I always forget. The rough-cut look may be acceptable in the barn, but it doesn't impress judges -- at least not favorably.

"Next time borrow my scissors; they're sharper," quipped one amused breeder when he saw my does.

"Scissors?" scoffed my husband. "She just needs to sharpen her teeth."

"Hah, hah. You're a riot, dear. Why don't you just remind me to sharpen the clipper blades?"

In earlier years, before I bought two new clippers, one for bodies and a smaller one for udders and legs, I had more problems than just dull blades. My first clipper was old when I was born. And I was no young kid when I found it at a garage sale -- cheap. The darn thing was so noisy and heavy, after clipping one goat I was exhausted and deaf. So was the goat.

I did have a small clipper for udders and ears: a secondhand, inexpensive model -- virtually powerless. The little thing ran fine until it came across hair. I averaged one hour per udder. That's a yearling udder. Older, full-sized does took longer. Especially if they objected, which they always did.

When goats resist, I tend to say bad words. Or cry. Neither one would do much for the image of goat breeders, so I do my clipping at home, away from the public. Anyhow, I couldn't have taken my goliath clippers to a show. With those things roaring, no one could have carried on a conversation in the same county. And I would have died before I'd let anyone watch me clip legs. Since my small clipper was not powerful enough to do anything with hair on it, I was stuck with trying to trim delicate little pasterns (ankles) with a clipper the size of a scuba tank.

Now and then, in spite of my clippers, a doe ended up looking rather good. But that sort of doe was one who would probably look even better unclipped.

A young woman came up to me after a show and asked: "Your doe looks so sleek and shiny. What number blade did you use on her?" I choked, sputtered, and finally said: "Uh, it's a plucking blade. Yes, that's it! A plucking blade." I knew there was such a thing, because I'd seen it in catalogs.

My does would have agreed. They were convinced the blade I used plucked rather than cut. Not true. As long as the blade was sharp, my archaic clipper cut rather well if I kept dipping it in the mixture of oil and gas my husband made for me. Or was it oil and kerosene? Oil and diesel? When Johnny wasn't around, I just went out to his shop and poured a little of this and that into the dip can.

I've noticed that my new clippers warn against using anything but specially formulated clipper oil for lubricating the blades. Maybe that's why the old clipper sounded so funny. A neighbor even stopped by once to ask where the helicopter was.

"You must have heard these clippers I use on my goats," I told him, and I turned them on to demonstrate.

"Good grief," he hollered, with his hands over his ears. "What do they run on? Diesel?"

TEST DAY

Many of us diehard goat crazies participate in official DHIA testing. (Dairy Herd Improvement Association, or Dairymen Hoping to Impress *Anyone.*) Once a month someone comes to our farm, weighs each doe's milk and takes a sample of it, which is then sent to a lab for butterfat analysis. A computer compiles the milk record for each goat based on these monthly tests, and the national goat registry publishes yearly books listing these records. Many goat breeders use these records in their advertisements. I don't, but I'm "on test" anyhow. I'm not sure why. For "genetic progress", maybe? Or "herd management"? Or, how about, "the helluvit"?

Years ago I was on "group test", where herd owners test each other's goats... and trade gossip about other goat herds. Now I'm on "standard test", where one person is hired to test several herds... and convey gossip. Both types of testing produce anxiety in herd owners, who want their goats to do well. After all, if other breeders are going to talk about our animals, we want them to have only nice things to say. "Linda's animals certainly milk well, don't they?" And things like that. Unfortunately, goats never milk as well as they "should" on test day.

Having been both a milk production tester and testee, I have amassed a wealth of excuses for low production on test day. "She milked eight pounds last night," I blithely inform the tester as I sit down to milk. "But she always drops for test." She dropped all right. About four pounds. "Maybe the new batch of feed upset her," I rationalize. "Or maybe she's in heat." (In May?)

9

"Are you sure," I ask my tester, who's heard it all before, "that you read the scales right?"

I don't outright lie about my goats' milking abilities, but I do tend to exaggerate. I seem to remember milk weights from days I stumble out to the barn two hours late better than weights taken after exactly twelve hours. (Goats are generally milked twice a day. Although some dairymen milk *three* times a day. Such people are to be held in awe, like people who brush their teeth after every meal.)

When I keep daily milk records, I remember highs better than the average amounts. A goat who milks 8.6, 8.2, 7.8, 9.1, and 8.4 is obviously a 9 pound milker. She was just a bit "off" the other four days. And a doe who milks 7 pounds is a gallon milker, even though a gallon of milk weighs 8.6 pounds. The reason is simple. Any goat over a year old should be able to milk a gallon a day. If she milks 7 pounds and I want to keep her, 7 pounds is a gallon. This isn't lying, it's accommodating.

I strongly suspect other breeders are no different, because I have yet to buy a 12 pound milker who gave more than 8 pounds of milk. Granted, she did change homes, feed, and owners, which is highly traumatic, but goats I sell often go up in production for their new owners. I've never decided if that's because the new owners feed better or lie more.

While on group test, I ran across a lot of heavy milkers who lightened up considerably every test day. I'm fairly creative when it comes to explaining away precipitous drops in milk, but I learned excuses from other goatkeepers that I had never dreamed of.

"My husband milked yesterday. That always throws the girls into a tizzy." (Is he extremely handsome, I wonder?)

"I have a splitting headache." (Presumably, the does hold up their milk in empathy.)

Some breeders get personal: "Super Milk Molly knows the sound of your car. She holds up her milk as soon as you turn in the driveway." Or worse yet: "My goats always drop in milk when you test us. You must smell different." I also look and sound different, why not pick on those characteristics?

Most breeders don't need such exotic excuses -- anything will do. "I gave the goats inoculations yesterday," or "trimmed their feet" or "dewormed them." Everyone knows if a doe's routine is varied by so much as a blink of an eye, her milk production will drop in half...as it will if she comes in heat -- which every goat does, beginning in August, every test day. Amazing, since goats are seasonal breeders.

Many of my excuses are obviously legitimate. "My does would do much better if I milked on time every day...They've dropped because I forgot to fill their water buckets...Maybe if I bought some alfalfa..."

Those breeders whose management is superb -- who feed free-choice alfalfa, a good dairy ration, milk precisely on time, keep herd-health chores up-to-date and have soft music playing all day in the barn -- must look harder than I do for excuses for test-day deficits. They rise to the challenge magnificently.

"My teenaged son changed radio stations yesterday and subjected my does to four hours of hard rock. No wonder they're not milking."

That's one excuse I could accept. I had more trouble with this one: "The girls are nervous today. They just don't milk well when they're nervous. I'll bet they don't like my new coveralls."

Or this one: "My goats drop in milk whenever they sense a change in the weather. It's awfully cloudy today. I'll bet it rains tomorrow."

But my all-time favorite excuse comes from one "super manager" I tested. "My girls are accustomed to being milked precisely on time. You are one and a half minutes late," she scolded. "They've reabsorbed their milk."

TAKING PICTURES
AND PULLING TEETH

Taking pictures of goats ranks right up there with having teeth pulled. I put it off as long as possible because it's so painful.

Every year I tell myself that I'm going to photograph my goats properly. At shows. When they're clipped, clean and uddered up. Every year, at shows, when the goats are clipped, clean and uddered up, I'm too hysterical to take pictures.

"Not now!" I scream as my partner, camera in hand, gently suggests the time has come. "I don't want to stress them before the show." After the show, I want to get them milked as soon as possible -- they've already been uddered up too long.

Consequently, all the pictures I have are of dry, pregnant goats in fuzzy, winter coats lounging next to the manure pile -- comfortable, unstressed... and ugly. (Dry does are those who are not milking and therefore udderless. Udderless goats are as attractive to goat buyers as udderless women are to men.)

One year, I tried. I really did. Since kids run on their dams, the only day the does have full udders (other than at shows) is on test day, when kids are locked away. So one fine summer morning, half an hour before the tester was due to arrive, my good-natured husband followed me to the barn to take pictures. I held the goat. He worked the camera.

"Tell me when you're ready," he said. I set up Phoebe as best I could -- she really needed more than eleven-and-a-half hours of milk to look her best. (Twenty-four hours would have helped.)

"Okay. Now!" I ordered, stepping back.

Johnny had forgotten to cock the shutter. In the second it took to discover his mistake and correct it, Phoebe crossed her front legs and swayed her back. We tried again.

This time she moved her back legs. "Her udder doesn't show up," Johnny complained, peering through the view finder.

"I can't help that," I snapped. "I can't give her a silicone implant. Just take it!"

For the next doe, Johnny positioned the goat while I operated the camera. I had no trouble seeing Wanda's huge udder. Unfortunately, I also had no trouble seeing her steep rump.

"Get her back down, please." (I was trying to give orders politely.)

"How?" my husband asked.

"Like this." I demonstrated the stroke-the-loin technique. Wanda dutifully crouched under my touch, flexing her back legs and straightening her topline. However, when Johnny tried, she walked away.

"Hold her still!" I bellowed. My politeness was wearing off.

After several minutes of attempting, unsuccessfully, to set Wanda up according to my specifications, Johnny grabbed the camera and handed me the goat. "YOU do it!"

By then, Wanda was in no mood to cooperate. It was milking time, and she was tired of being prodded and poked. I gave up. The next goat was even less willing to be photographed. I was irritable. Johnny wanted to leave for work. Fortunately, the tester drove up, giving us an excuse to quit before our marriage, as well as the photo session, unraveled.

The only photos we got were of Phoebe, sway-backed with her legs crossed, and of Wanda dragging Johnny across the driveway.

At the very last show of the year, a friend who takes excellent goat photographs volunteered to take pictures for me, so I could run ads with pictures.

We're still friends. But we didn't get many photos.

"That's enough, she's getting upset," I pleaded after the first picture.

"Calm down, Linda. You need photos. Right?"

"Yes, but it's too sunny out here -- she'll overheat. It's too windy, she'll get chilled. Anyway, I'm a nervous wreck."

"Okay, Okay. We'll get pictures right after you come out of the ring."

Right after we came out of the ring, I put the goats on the milkstand.

"Wait!" my friend begged.

"No, I can't stand it," I whimpered. "I want to get them milked." My poor friend snapped rear udder shots while I milked.

"I see why you don't have any photos of your goats," she sighed.

I'm considering running ads with candid shots. I have several blurry ones of my husband throwing himself across a goat to stop her from leaving the scene. I also have a few of goats on their hind legs, goats scratching, going pee and poop, and posing in a variety of contorted positions.

How other people make their goats stand like statues, I'll never know. The only time mine are motionless is when they're asleep by the manure pile -- hairy, pregnant and dry.

"Just take my word for it," I tell prospective customers who write asking for photos. "My does are beautiful, but they're camera shy. Getting them in a photograph is like pulling teeth."

My teeth.

JUDGING JUDGES

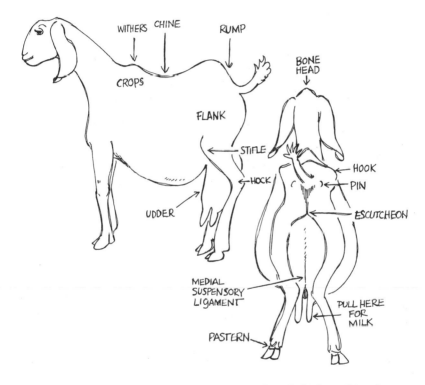

During goat show season, judges' clichés flit about as thick as flies on a manure pile. Goat judges go through a rigorous training program, where they learn to evaluate goats on the basis of "dairy character", "body capacity", "general appearance" and "mammary system" (udder). They are taught specific phrases like "deeper in the flank" and "more open in the ribs" to explain their placings.

However, put a microphone in a judge's hand at a goat show and look out. That judge's pet phrases will soon outnumber the ones he was taught. Some judges like "substance of bone", others "refinement". What these terms mean is anybody's guess.

Then there are the judges who want every doe to walk "uphill". It took some time before I realized uphill goats are those whose withers are higher than their rumps. It wasn't until I saw exhibitors dragging goats around the ring with their front feet two inches off the ground that I understood.

That method of showing also works for the judge who loves "long, lean necks". Although it would be easier to just substitute giraffes.

And there are the "flat bone" specialists. "Notice the flatness of bone, especially in the legs." Sorry, I DON'T notice, not even when I peer intently. Anyhow, who wants flat legs? Round ones are sturdier, it seems to me. Unfortunately, most of my goats are so fat, you can't find their bones -- flat or round.

And that's another place where judges differ -- on fat. The first day of a two day show all the big hunks will be at the end of the line for lacking "refinement and dairy character". The next day, under a different judge, they're at the top for "substance and body capacity". That's why I like two day shows -- everyone gets a chance.

A judge in our area placed one doe over another for an advantage in "skeletal integrity". Skeletal integrity??? Maybe the doe behind her had a broken rib.

In addition to unique terminology, each judge has his/her unique ringside manner. Some are polite to all exhibitors. They find something nice to say about the goat at the end of the line, even if she's built like a 2 X 4 on a sawbuck and her udder looks like two light bulbs dangling from a smashed pear. "This doe, though standing in last place, must be commended for her adequate breed character". In other words, she looks like a goat.

Others are less tactful. Such as a judge who commented on the last three does in a line up.

"There's nothing down here that several years and a few good bucks couldn't help." Or the judge who said, "This is the wrong kind of Nubian -- just what we *don't* want." She was talking about my goat -- the one that went Junior Champion the day before.

Worse yet are those judges who answer questions with brutal honesty. One exhibitor, whose goats had placed poorly all day, asked the judge: "What would you do if you had my herd?"

His response -- "Mister, I'd load my gun." If the exhibitor had taken the judge's advice, the first bullet would have been aimed at the judge.

Sometimes you learn something from listening to judges. However, knowing that your doe is "fuller in the crops" than the doe behind her doesn't do much good if you don't know where "the crops" are (is?) Likewise, if the doe ahead is "more level from hooks to pins", you need to know that the judge is not talking about sewing notions.

We have a responsibility, as exhibitors, to learn the difference between an escutcheon, a stifle and a medial suspensory ligament. Then we'll sound intelligent when we knock a judge's reasons.

I do sympathize with the poor fools who stand up all day placing goats. It would be tough to keep doing your best and stay positive after a long day of comparing one squirming screaming kid to another. *Most* judges are very dedicated and conscientious.

But... I would love, just once, to have a class of judges parading around the ring while exhibitors gave reasons for placings.

"Judge 1 over Judge 2 for an advantage in Reasons, being more logical, consistent and accurate.

"Judge 2 over Judge 3 for a distinct advantage in Compassion Capacity, being much better able to get her point across without reducing an exhibitor to tears.

"Judge 3 over Judge 4 because of a decided advantage in Moral Character, being more concerned with the merits of the animal than who owns it."

And finally, "The judge standing in last place today, while a miserable example of the breed, must be commended for at least wearing a reasonably clean pair of pants."

GOAT ESCAPES

It's summertime! And "the corn is as high as an elephant's eye" -- or it was until the goats got out. The cherry tree had leaves on it before the goats escaped, too. It's amazing how much damage a dozen goats can do in as many minutes of freedom.

After an expensive building program, we now have excellent gates and fences. The problem is we have a doe, Gigi, who is a master at catching our spring-closed gates on the bounce. She waits for someone to go out and bang a gate behind. As the gate rebounds half-an-inch or so, she wedges her nose in the tiny gap. With a flick of her head, the gap widens and she's out! Her cohorts have learned to wait by her flank, then dash through with her.

Tossing their heads and leaping happily in the air, they dance their way to the corn patch, to the fruit trees, to whatever other forbidden fruit they can grab before I discover their escape and, screaming hysterically, chase them back in.

We had one poor little maple tree that developed all sorts of camouflage tactics to avoid its predators. When first planted, the maple was five feet tall with maybe six leaves way at the top. "This type of maple grows rapidly and will make a good shade tree for the barn," we were assured by the friend who gave it to us. The friend didn't take thirty goats and twenty sheep into account. After the first goat escape, the tree was broken off two feet from the ground. I figured it was a goner but the game little thing just branched from the bottom.

The maple made it through one season unscathed before a sheep escape denuded it. The next year, instead of growing up, it grew outward forming a tight clump of branches and leaves. For several years, only the outer leaves were nibbled. The inner ones were safely hidden. Then, one year, my whole herd of goats escaped and charged right over the top of the poor thing, breaking it off at ground level.

Another frequent victim of goat escapes is the cherry tree (the one that used to have leaves). For a while, it was contending with more than occasional escapes. One big dry doe routinely appeared outside her pen, munching the cherry tree. We couldn't find any holes in the fence and couldn't believe that blimp could jump out, but out she was -- every day.

20

At last, I caught her in the act. Way down at the far end of her pasture, where the new chain-link fence forms right angles with the old woven-wire crossfence, we had neglected to fasten the wire to the post. With her massive body, Gigi pushed the woven-wire out and walked around the post. The wire sprang back into place behind her. Some goat.

However, if I deliberately open wide a gate and invite the goats to come for a romp, they dash to the far side of the field and stand quivering, as though I were asking them to climb into a slaughterhouse truck.

One day a visitor came to see Gigi, the gate-opening goat. I took Gigi by the collar and tried to lead her through the same gate she's always bullying her way through. That crazy goat planted her feet and refused to budge. After several minutes of futilely pulling her this way and that, I gave up and stalked out the gate, slamming it behind me. The gate bounced back, Gigi caught it, and instantly the visitor and I were bowled over by a dozen happily escaping goats. At that moment, chevon stew seemed too good a fate for those does.

Johnny has the same feelings, I'm sure, when I'm at a goat show and he's stuck at home with the chores. Our goats know the milking order and come in properly for me. However, when anyone else milks, my does are disobedient and unruly, like a class of kids with a substitute teacher. Open the door and they all charge in, scrambling for position on the milk stand, tipping over buckets, and generally creating chaos.

When I return, I'm always afraid to ask how things went.

"No problems," Johnny will say. "I killed off the troublemakers and the other two behaved fine."

Of course he's just teasing -- so far. But I'll bet our cherry tree wishes Johnny were serious. Before it meets the same fate as the maple, it should try disguising itself as a large tube of deworming paste. That ought to keep the goats away.

Alas, trees, as far as I know, cannot convert themselves into tubes of deworming paste, so I'm afraid our cherry tree's days are numbered. But when that tree's number comes up, I'll bet it waits to topple until it can clobber a marauding goat on the way down.

CHANGE OF HEART

It's strange how suddenly Johnny can change his mind about a goat. Take Gigi, for instance. She left my herd as a three-month-old doeling and was raised by a family with five rambunctious children. Gigi learned how to take care of herself. At the age of six, when her family moved to town, she came back to me. For more than a year, she had been running free with a flock of sheep in a several hundred acre pasture. Gigi did not take kindly to being confined to a barn and feedlot with twenty goats. She did learn rather quickly which door led to the milk-room and grain. And how to open the door. If someone happened to be standing in the way -- too bad. For a while, large Gigi hoofprints beat a regular path across my feet and even, at times, my prone body. Gigi is a large, bullheaded goat.

Johnny doesn't like pushy goats. He especially doesn't like goats that push HIM. Since Gigi is not choosy about whom she pushes, she and Johnny quickly developed an adversarial relationship.

"How do you expect me to put corn husks in the feeder with this two ton cow blocking my way? ...Ouch! #!*%! GET OFF MY FOOT!!"

Gigi never did learn to wait patiently for Johnny to walk from door to manger. If he held the husks too high for her to reach, she'd walk up the front of him until he and the husks were lower.

"Why do you keep this obnoxious ox?" he'd ask.

After she freshened, the reason was obvious. Her udder was beautiful. Unfortunately, her personality didn't change. But she did grow fond of me. She even quit stepping on my feet and knocking me down in her haste to jump on the milkstand. Or maybe I just learned to stay out of her way. After a few years, she showed affection to everyone -- rubbing her head on any available behind. But Johnny wasn't impressed. She still tried to go through him if he happened to be between her and food. She's always had a terrific appetite.

Then came her ninth year. Gigi was more beautiful than ever. And more bullheaded. She had chalked up ten grand champion wins. But Johnny still disliked her. Until the last day of the Oregon State Fair.

Earlier in the week, Gigi, three-quarters Nubian and one-quarter Alpine, won Grand Champion Recorded

Grade. Johnny arrived on the last day of the fair to help me load and bring everybody home. First, however, was the Best-Doe-In-Show class. Gigi had been through many of these, never winning. Recorded Grades seem to have a tough time in Best-In-Show classes.

However, this time, her age impressed the judge, and, to my great surprise, Gigi won. As she led me back to her pen, I heard Johnny tell admiring fairgoers, "This goat of ours is the best goat in the whole barn. Yep. She's the best there is."

Over and over all evening, as unsuspecting people walked by, Johnny accosted them and said, "See that big brown goat over there? She was named Supreme Champion this afternoon. Yup. She's the best goat here."

I tried to shush him, but it was no use. He was as proud as if he'd sired her himself.

When we loaded the does for the homeward journey, Gigi, as usual, stepped on Johnny's feet. He grimaced and bit his lip, while I cringed, waiting for the customary fusillade of unprintable words. Instead, he managed a painful smile and muttered through clenched teeth: "That's okay. She didn't mean to. Get in there you big Best-Doe-In-Show, you."

Ever since then, whenever one of my goats plows into Johnny while he's trying to feed, or bowls him over when he's trying to load, I placate him with: "I know she's difficult. But I think she's as good as Gigi. She might even go Best-In-Show some day at the Oregon State Fair."

TRIPPING
TO THE BARN

On summer days, I trip to the barn later than usual...and I do mean "trip". Gardening, hauling hay, canning and other late summer chores keep me busy until after dark. When at last I have the bucket of pig slops in one hand and milk pail in the other, I'm too tired to remember what I left lying around between house and barn. I find out soon enough, as I crash into the wheelbarrow, or stumble over a hoe. As many times as

I've been bathed in potato peels and moldy left-overs, you'd think I'd remember to keep equipment off the path.

But even if I were to remember, someone else would leave a booby trap. Like the rabbit trap. A domestic rabbit that escaped and refused to be caught settled into our garden. Our two sons, Kevin and Steve, youngsters then, made a chicken wire fence designed to funnel the little corn-muncher into the chicken yard. Alas, their fence ran across my trail to the barn.

Every evening my spouse would remind me to "watch out for the rabbit trap." And I did. Carefully feeling my way to the fence, I stepped over and proceeded to the barn. But...after finishing chores, I trudged wearily back to the house, oblivious to everything -- including the fence...which hit me at shin height every night and sent me and the milk sprawling. Since the only thing that fence ever trapped was me and, one late night, my husband on the tractor, the boys dismantled it. I went back to just stumbling over hoes, pitchforks and other paraphernalia.

I could carry a flashlight -- in my teeth, since my hands are full -- but why should I when I know where I'm going? The barn has lights. The house has lights. I just have to navigate the few hundred feet between them. I know that path so well I could walk it in my sleep -- and usually do. If junk would stay out of my way, I'd be fine.

But junk won't. One late night, after carefully removing the pitchfork that nearly knocked me out the night before when I stepped on its tines, I started confidently toward the barn with my bucket of peach peels and trimmings. The peaches were canned, the path was free (or so I thought), and all was well in my world. Until my right foot met the spokes on the front wheel of Steve's reclining bicycle. The wheel changed positions abruptly under the weight of my firmly entangled foot, throwing me sideways and backwards onto the bike, with a gallon of slimy peach peels oozing over me.

The family arrived quickly at the scene, wondering what all the noise was about.

"Hey, Mom, you bent the spokes on my bike," wailed my son.

"I bent the spokes on your bike?" I repeated through clenched teeth, as I tried to convince my foot to face the same direction as the rest of my leg.

"Yeah. Just look at it!"

"Would you help me up, please, dear?" I asked my husband. "I'm going to kill your son."

"Don't let her touch me, dad! She's all slimy!"

To save my milk production tester from bicycles and other dangers on our path, I lead the way to the barn. She follows the reflection from my pig bucket. If the reflection careens wildly, the tester knows she'd better stop and wait for me to pick myself off the ground and move the obstruction. Sometimes, she remembers to bring a flashlight. She didn't have one the night she met a barn owl, but a light wouldn't have helped.

Barn owls are useful birds, eating mice and other pesky rodents. However, the one residing in our barn has a nasty habit of swooping invisibly in front of us while emitting an unearthly shriek. I never get used to that noise. I know when I get a certain distance from the barn, an owl is going to fly out of the loft and shriek. But when it does, I jump.

I forgot to warn the tester. She never saw his ghostly shape in the darkness. She just heard a piercing, raucous scream directly above her. Her scream doubled his in intensity as she flung herself around my neck.

"Good heavens," she gasped. "What was that?!"

"A barn owl," I squeaked. "I forgot to tell you he does that every night." I was squeaking partly from my own terror, but mostly because her fingers were cutting off my wind. "It's okay," I rasped faintly. "He's friendly."

"Well, he has a heckuva way of showing it," she retorted, climbing off my back.

"Would you mind unwrapping your fingers now?" I croaked. "He's gone."

"Oh, sorry...It's just that I never heard an owl that sounded like that. I thought they said "hoo hoo"."

"Great horned owls do. Barn owls just scream," I informed her between grateful gulps of air.

"Then I wish you'd change owls...unless you want to find yourself another tester."

I don't want to find another tester; I doubt I could considering the conditions. But I don't know how to "change owls" either. Maybe my tester will get used to screeches in the dark. I'll take screeches over wheelbarrows any day. If I let her go first next time, she'll realize how lucky she is to contend with nothing more than unearthly noises.

First, though, I'd better buy her a miner's hat with lamp attached; I don't want her breaking a leg on my path. I'd like one of those hats, too. It would be better than trying to aim a flashlight gripped in my teeth. And if a bicycle gets left on the path again, a lamp could save my life... and my son's.

SURVIVAL
OF THE FITTEST

My vet doesn't see much of me anymore -- to the relief of everyone in his office. He's very good with goats, and amazingly patient with goat owners, but I'm a difficult case. Having a background in zoology, I know just enough to question every move he makes... but not always enough to understand the answers. And so he's trapped between not daring to "talk down" to me, yet not wanting to embarrass me by talking over my head. Add to that situation my neurotic Nubians' natural aversion to vets, and my own queer ideas of goat health care, and you have a perfect formula for creating ulcers in even the most mellow veterinarian.

When I decided, some years ago, to quit doctoring and let natural selection take over, my good-natured vet just shook his head in wonder. "I suppose that IS an alternative," he said. Not, I'm sure, a very intelligent alternative to a man schooled in treating disease. However, it has worked fine for me. Sickly does don't live to produce more sickly does. The survivors are delightfully healthy. They have to be. Oh, I still vaccinate, deworm, and give Bo-Se shots, but not mouth-to-mouth resuscitation or other extraordinary life-saving measures.

Well, usually. Although, theoretically, I treat all animals equally, some animals are more equal than others. When my prize doe, Total Eclipse, came up lame the day before a show, I dashed her to the vet.

"Well, well. What are YOU doing here?"

The vet suspected a fractured bone in the joint above the pastern, but said the only way to know for sure was to x-ray the leg.

"We'll just lay her on her side on the table with her leg stretched out straight, take one shot in that position, then roll her onto her belly and get a shot at a different angle."

I looked at him. I looked at the waist-high stainless steel table he indicated. And I looked at my 175 pound goat. As far as I could tell, "we" consisted of him, his assistant/wife, and me. Surely he didn't expect a big, strong, full-grown goat to allow three paltry humans to plop her down on a cold, hard piece of steel three feet in the air? Alas, he did indeed.

To move her into position, the vet gave Total a sideways push. Unfortunately, she moved onto his wife's foot. His wife was wearing open-toed sandals. As she writhed in pain, trying valiantly to hold back the tears and the words she must certainly have been thinking, he asked, "Are you okay?". When she could, she nodded. The vet must have thought "okay" meant "fine", instead of "alive", because he said, "Then let's get her up here."

Such sympathy. I would have hit him over the head with a microscope, but the vet's wife just collected herself, pulled her feet as far out of harm's way as possible, and prepared for action.

Action we got. Total turned every which way but inside out. Somehow, we held on and wrestled her onto the table. As we all lay draped, panting, over the wildly thrashing goat, desperately trying to hold down various moving parts, the vet hollered for his receptionist:

"Shelley, we're going to need your help!"

"Really?" came the surprised reply. Evidently she wasn't often called upon to assist in handling animals.

Struggling to keep Total's injured leg still and her body on the table, the vet bellowed with considerably more volume and urgency, "SHELLEY, GET IN HERE!!" That yielded results.

The four of us managed to get Total calmed down and one x-ray picture taken. We all realized the futility of rolling her onto her belly for another shot. With much less struggle, we lowered her to the ground. I think, by that time, she'd decided we were all nuts and the best thing to do was humor us.

The x-ray showed a hair-line fracture, and so we moved outside for the cast-building procedure. That went a bit more smoothly, with only a few false starts as Total indignantly stomped the gooey strip of bandage into the concrete. My vet talked as he worked, explaining everything he did before I had a chance to ask questions. He needn't have worried; all my energy was directed toward keeping Total more-or-less still.

The completed cast hardened quickly, and soon my disgusted goat was safely loaded in the van. As I drove away, I seemed to hear a collective sigh of relief from the battered trio left behind.

Six weeks later, I called for an appointment to get the cast removed. Strangely, the vet suggested we give it another week. When I arrived for the appointment, I noticed that everyone was wearing steel-toed boots.

The vet complimented me on how dry and clean I had kept the cast. I explained that goats don't like mud and are not nearly so messy as cows, so it's not hard to keep pens clean and dry. Well, that was wonderful. At least it was wonderful until he tried to cut the cast off. It was like concrete. The vet had applied many layers of plaster of paris, since he figured my rambunctious goat would beat half of them off. Not at all. She had learned, within the first five minutes of being reunited with the herd, that she could use her cast as a weapon, so I'd moved her to separate quarters. For seven weeks Total had been getting exclusive and preferential treatment and loving every minute of it. Far from damaging her cast, she had, apparently, taken special care of it.

The cast was not coming off without a battle -- its own and Total's. Soon the vet was using a chisel as well as the diamond-saw cutter. Total was convinced the grinding and chipping noises she heard were coming from her leg bones, and she wasn't standing still for THAT. It was a hot summer day, and, by the time the deed was done, we were all drenched.

Wearily, the vet helped me load my still limping goat into the van, explaining it would be two weeks before we'd know if the bone had healed properly. In three weeks, Total was back to careening off the walls on a leg as good as new.

I don't think my vet and his assistants ever recovered completely from the "Total" ordeal. I know his wife doesn't wear open-toed sandals to the clinic anymore. But he still treats goats... when he can't get out of it.

A few months after the Total episode, I received this phone call spoken in a slow drawl:

"'Lo, Mizzuz Fink? I called the vet 'bout this here goat of mine what seems to be hoppin' 'round on three legs. She's a big, ornery Nubian. He said I should talk to you afore I decide to bring 'er in and ask ya 'bout some kinda new-fangled theory on treatin' goats. Somethin' called 'natural selection'?".

GOAT MYTHS

I resent cartoons of horned, hairy goats eating tin cans while nearby skunks hold their noses. I would love to improve the dairy goat image. I would love to, but my goats are not cooperating.

At fairs, after I explain at length to a young woman that goats are very fastidious and picky eaters, one of my does leans over the fence and nibbles on her plastic shopping bag. I quickly define the difference between eating and just tasting out of curiosity, the way a child touches everything, but the woman smiles skeptically, extricates her shirttail from another doe's mouth, and walks on -- more convinced than ever that goats will eat anything.

At every fair, helpful bystanders warn goat owners that one of their goats is eating a metal tack trunk, lawn chair, or milk stand. I'm going to paint on top of my tack trunk these words:

"My goats are *not* eating this trunk. They mouth it out of boredom, or to attract attention, but they do not *eat* it. I know. I've hauled *this same trunk* to goat shows for 15 years." I don't expect anyone except other goat owners to believe me.

Attitudes about goats start early in life. My goats have taught many youngsters the "truth" about goat-eating habits. A 6-year-old climbs up on the pen and asks, "Will they bite?"

"No," I answer. "But if you put your fingers in their mouths, you may feel teeth -- and that could hurt. Just pet them."

So the child leans over to pet a friendly goat, putting the buttons of his shirt directly in front of her nose. She, of course, nibbles on the buttons.

"Hey, she's eating my shirt!"

"No, she's just curious."

"Huh uh... Goats eat anything."

"Nonsense," I counter, determined to nip this misconception in the bud. "They eat hay and grain."

The child picks up a handful of dirty straw and wood shavings that has escaped from the pen into the aisle and offers it to the goat, who, being polite, pretends to nibble on the edges. At that moment, the boy's mother comes along and tells him to put that dirty straw down.

"Goats like dirty straw, Mommy. They'll eat anything."

What chance do I have against the certainty of a 6-year-old?

Then there's the one-time goat owner who comes by to reminisce about the "billy" he used to have. "Man, did he stink. I staked him in the blackberry thicket and he ate his way out. That goat would eat anything he could reach." I'd like to stake that man in the middle of a blackberry bush. After a week, he'd eat anything he could reach, too.

The smelly-goat prejudice is just as difficult to change. I've heard mothers at fairs tell their children, "Don't touch the goats. They stink."

"No, they don't, Ma'am," I correct politely. "Only the males smell during the fall breeding season. Come see."

Doubtfully, she steps closer. Not noticing anything offensive, she pats one gently on the head. Later, I'm sure, she tells her children that most goats stink, but these have been cleaned up for the fair.

My Nubian bucks are not very odiferous... out in the cool barn... in early spring. Some visitors hardly notice the scent, and sometimes pet the friendly fellows -- on the head -- before I can warn them. Then they wipe their hands on their pants. Once inside a warm room, the essence of buck is quite noticeable indeed. My visitors go away convinced that goats stink.

Since everyone in my neighborhood knows I raise goats, I try very hard not to smell like a buck when I go to town. I'm not always successful. After handling the buck, I shower and scrub and put on clean clothes. Then, with 15 minutes to get to a meeting, I hear pandemonium coming from the barn. I dash out to find the doe I just bred to one buck, climbing the wall into another buck's pen. I drag her back and lock her out of harm's way. She, of course, has not showered and scrubbed since her rendezvous with Buck Number 1. I now smell like a buck again with no time to change.

If the image of goats is to change, I fear my goats and I are not the ones to change it. Only by owning dairy goats themselves will people learn how clean are goats and how discriminating their tastes. New goat owners learn that switching goats from rolled grains to pellets precipitates a hunger strike. Even altering the amount of molasses in the grain mix can throw them off feed for days.

But I'll never convince a spectator at the fair that goats are finicky, when he sees mine eating the clean straw as soon as I throw it down, while their feeder full of alfalfa is ignored. Nevertheless, I'll keep trying. "They taste whatever is new," I explain. "But goats actually prefer good quality hay and grain."

"Oh, really?" remarks the fairgoer. "Your goat just ate my swirl fries."

BREEDING SEASON

C-DAY
AND THE FASTEST
BUCK IN THE WEST

The bucks and I used to look forward to breeding season, for different reasons, of course. I enjoyed planning which does to breed to which bucks to produce kids better than their dams. The bucks enjoyed implementing my plans -- and some of their own.

Since the advent of artificial insemination, we've all lost some of our enthusiasm. Oh, the bucks still get natural services occasionally, but they also get their semen collected for posterity -- and that's not fun... for any of us.

"To insure the highest quality and quantity of semen, be sure your bucks are flushed well before collection day (C-Day to me), but let them rest for a few days just prior to collection."

So state the instructions from one collector. Sounds innocent enough, doesn't it? And those directions would be simple to follow if my does cooperated by coming into heat every three days, instead of every three weeks, before C-Day. But they don't. And so I'm stuck with the unhappy alternative to a doe in heat -- the artificial vagina (AV).

I don't care to go into the operation of an AV in detail. Suffice it to say, it's not the most pleasant way to spend a hot autumn day, unless you happen to enjoy the intimate company of bucks in full, malodorous rut. I don't.

Flushing a buck requires the services of both me and an unwilling doe. Things would be a lot simpler if someone around here would help hold the doe -- but they all disappear when the AV comes out of the closet. And so I must convince some incredulous doe to stand quietly while I flag her tail and a buck jumps on her back. Sure.

Failing in that, I must convince the buck that the doe that is lunging, rearing, screaming, and, very likely, flipping upside down in front of him, is actually a doe in heat just waiting to be mounted.

"You've got to be kidding," say most of my bucks. They take one look and leave.

Then there was Hondo. After many years of flushings and collections, Hondo was accustomed to the AV. He really didn't need a doe at all. Just let him out of his pen and get ready. He'd mount the nearest object -- be it doe, fence post, or an onlooker's leg. Made no difference to him. That could sometimes be a problem, depending on how understanding the onlooker was.

It could also be disastrous on C-Day, if the collector wasn't prepared. Hondo, as an old buck, had good quality semen, but not much of it. A collector could not afford to miss a single one of Hondo's ejaculations. Unfortunately, they almost all did, often more than one. A typical session would go like this:

"Are you ready?" I ask, poised by Hondo's gate.

"Sure, sure, let him out," responds the confident collector.

I open the gate, grab for a collar, miss; Hondo heads for the doe as the collector takes his position at her side...

Oops.

"Need a rag for your knee?" I ask solicitously.

Fortunately, goat folks don't get uptight about such things. Unfortunately, not all my friends are goat folks. Some are city folk, for whom a buck is a dollar bill.

There's nothing I dread more than the thought of one of my sophisticated city friends coming to visit when I'm out in the barn flushing bucks. Well, maybe one thing would be worse; if Johnny were home when they came. I can hear the conversation now:

"Hello, Johnny, and what is Linda doing this morning?"

He smiles wickedly and answers... in dramatic detail.

THE TRUTH ABOUT A-I

Most dairy goat breeders have read articles about what a Great Thing artificial insemination is, and how, with a few simple lessons, You, Too, can impregnate your does with super semen. I've read those glowing reports. And I'm here to tell you that anyone who thinks A-I is easy either: 1) has never tried it; 2) has been doing it for 20 years and has forgotten what his first attempts were like; or 3) was born with the agility of Houdini, the patience of Job, and the coordination of a neurosurgeon. I know. I've been there.

Now I don't want Ida and Andy Purcella to get their feelings hurt. They did their best with me, they really did. And during their A-I course I felt pretty confident. I could find the cervix, and I could even gently manipulate a pipette through those cervical folds. But, let's face it, a dry run is never quite like the real thing.

I checked the mucus on my doe regularly; the right time finally arrived. I dashed off to the neighbor's to get my semen from his tank. Thawing it in water at the correct temperature, warming the gun, counting seconds, propping the doe's abdomen on my knee, leaning over and around to insert the speculum, fastening the battery-operated light... oh, drat, why won't the light work NOW, of all times... Jiggle, jiggle... Ah, there it is. Okay, all systems are go. But... I can't hang on to the speculum while loading the gun and straw into the pipette. Oh, well, the doe is just standing here.

Oh, no! She coughed!

Do you have any idea what happens when a goat coughs while a glass speculum is resting, unattended, in her back end? Well, let me describe the scene: the speculum shoots out like a bullet from a gun barrel, crashes into the wall and shatters into a million pieces.

"Calm down," I tell myself.

"Live and learn, right? Ha,ha."

Another speculum... This time I hold on. Okay, locate the cervix... where is that thing, anyway? There goes the light again!

"Oh, hi, Johnny. Could you jiggle those batteries? I can't get the light to work. ...Thanks.

"What am I doing? Inseminating this doe, what does it look like?

"*Never mind!* Johnny, please. This is serious business. I'm creating a future champion."

"No, now that you mention it, I'm not comfortable. Maybe if I shift her weight a little... *Oh no!* (expletives deleted)" She coughed again. This time speculum, gun, pipette, and straw all came shooting out and splattered across the floor, walls, everywhere.

"No, Johnny, I cannot scoop the semen up and put it back in. Now would you please go away and let me cry in peace?"

My next attempt went more smoothly. The doe didn't cough, for one thing. And I did manage to deposit the semen in the proper place at what, I thought, was the proper time. However, the doe came back in heat 20 days later. So I threw in the towel, among other things, and gave her to the buck, which is what SHE wanted all along.

I didn't let one failure sour me on A-I forever. And I certainly don't want to discourage anyone else. However, I think it's only fair to tell you the truth about A-I. Don't be fooled by those magazine articles that make it sound as easy as scratching your back. The people who write them can no doubt scratch between their own shoulder blades both over and under-handed. AND they have partners who support the does and hang on to speculums. *My* partner has all he can do to support his own weight while he hangs on to his side laughing.

That's all right. I'm much better at A-I now. Not only have I not lost any more speculums, quite a few goats in my herd are the end results of my inseminations. If I had enough nerve, I'd wear a hat like A-I instructor Ida Purcella's:

SOCIAL REJECT

I don't realize how far removed I am, as a goat breeder, from the rest of society until breeding season arrives. (After I've been handling bucks, polite society wishes I were even *farther* removed.) Although I don't spend as much time smelling like an overexcited buck as I used to (thanks to artificial insemination), I still manage to fall into embarrassing predicaments.

Like when I saw a friend in a supermarket line who innocently asked, "What are you doing this afternoon, Linda? Why don't you stop by and visit?"

"I'd love to," I hollered back to her, where she stood three lines over, "but I'm going over to John Doe's place this afternoon and pick up some semen."

The shocked look on my friend's face and the in-drawn breaths all around me were puzzling at first. So I repeated loudly, "I'M BUYING SEMEN FROM HIM."

Gasp. Cough. Gasp. Faces turned quickly away.

"To breed my *does*," I hurriedly added, as awareness began to seep into me. "My *goats*. You know, to breed them artificially."

"Yes, well. Heh heh," twittered my red-faced friend. "It's been nice seeing you. Bye now." And she turned her back and busied herself digging through her purse as though looking for something terribly important.

I guess most people don't discuss semen publicly. So why do they ask a goat breeder what she's doing of an afternoon, if they don't really want to know?

Then again, I needn't mention semen to get myself in trouble. When my 16-year-old son took his driver's license test at the county seat, 25 miles from our farm, my nitrogen tank and I went along. After his test, I planned to deliver semen to a goat breeder on the other side of town. My liquid nitrogen tank is housed in a large, plastic garbage can lined with foam to cushion it from sudden highway stops. (When I finally acquired my own expensive tank, I was determined to take good care of it.)

This contraption takes up the entire back area in our little station wagon. Since it quite severely limits visibility, I lifted the whole thing down onto the sidewalk outside the Department of Motor Vehicles, and stationed myself beside it, while Kevin took his driving test.

Most people walking by ignored me and my trash can. But every now and then, someone would start toward us as though to throw an apple core or cigarette butt in the garbage. Naturally, I moved closer still to my tank-disguised-as-a-garbage-can and put a protective arm around it. People seemed to change their minds when I did that, and walked quickly away.

One young man, chewing his lip nervously, came out of the DMV and headed for the drive test area. As he opened the door to his car, I turned my attention elsewhere. In a moment or two, I heard a noise beside me. Turning, I saw the nervous young man trying to pry the lid off my garbage can -- evidently to dispose of a sack of trash he must have had stashed in his car.

"Oh, no!" I exclaimed, grabbing for the lid. "This isn't a garbage can!"

The young man stared at me.

"It just looks like one," I added lamely. Then I removed the lid so he could see. When his eyes hit the metal cylindrical tank, padded carefully in foam, the color drained from his face. Slowly and cautiously, he backed away -- and tumbled off the curb. I'm afraid the poor fellow thought my nitrogen tank was a bomb. He jumped in his car and sped off without taking his driver's test. That's just as well. I don't think he would have passed. He jumped two curbs and was doing about ninety in a thirty-mile speed zone when I last saw him.

Even at home, I am confronted with the cultural differences between most people and goat breeders -- especially when houseguests arrive during breeding season. Non goat-breeders find my preoccupation with the heat cycles of goats rather peculiar. They seem vaguely embarrassed when I come bubbling in from the barn, announcing happily that Vanessa is coming into heat and should be ready to breed in the morning. They smile wanly and change the subject.

Houseguests with small children suffer the most from culture shock. Their children are fascinated by everything and love to share their excitement with parents.

"Mama, come see this daddy goat! Watch what he does. He's funny!" Mama is never amused. On the contrary, she's horrified. Buck goats, in their desire to attract mates, spray themselves with urine. This practice excites does in heat. It disgusts does who are not in heat. And people. Especially city people.

"Really, Linda. You should have warned me your barn was X-rated."

It's always a relief to be around goat people, after weeks of trying not to offend others. When a friend from Australia who runs a dairy cattle and goat operation in Queensland visited, I enjoyed comparing notes on A-I techniques between our two countries. His wife, although not a goat person, is accustomed to talk of mucus and semen thaw and insemination guns. She just ignored us. Like my husband, she has learned to live a normal life, in spite of being married to a social reject -- a goat breeder.

BARNERCIZE

Goat farmers are sitting on a potential gold-mine, and goodness knows we could use one. Very few goat owners make money. However, goat raising has a marketable by-product we've neglected: exercise.

That's right, exercise. Modern Man no longer stays in condition by chasing saber-toothed tigers, wrestling them to the ground, and dragging them home for supper. So he needs some other sort of exercise. Many Modern Men and Modern Women keep their muscles from atrophying by jogging or "working out". Modern Men and Modern Women pay good money to get pulled muscles.

Goat breeders, wake up. If health-seekers want to "work out", why not let them "work out" on our farms? Exercising in a country atmosphere beats jogging through city smog or in a boring gym. Jogging to the barn on a frosty morning, wearing weights in the form of milk pails, and jumping hurdles of abandoned bicycles and sleeping dogs is anything but boring. One never knows what sort of excitement awaits the early morning goat jogger... but, unlike city jogging, it probably won't be life-threatening. Goat breeders don't have to worry about being mugged running through a park. (Accosted by a buck in breeding season, perhaps, but not mugged).

And all those people jazzercizing themselves into a sweat could just as well "go for the burn" while hauling hay to music. Jazzercizers get only sore muscles for their efforts. What a waste. They could be getting sore muscles and a barn full of hay. It makes me weep to think of all the energy wasted in pointless exercise -- when it could be expended cleaning my barn.

Yes, *my* barn. Why not harness the wasted human energy of the world by forming goat farm health clubs? For a reasonable membership fee, people could have the privilege of milking, feeding, trimming feet and doing other fun and fat-reducing chores.

Health clubs tend to be social meccas -- but some people prefer solitude when they jiggle their blubber. We could schedule people either for group activities, like hay hauling, or solitary exercises, like trimming the buck's feet.

And exercises could be customized for each person's needs. If touching toes is called for, that person could pick up fallen apples to feed the goats. Stretching exercises? Pick the apples off the tree.

My heart warms at the thought of men and women strengthening their stomach muscles by hugging 100 pound sacks of feed and waddling to my feed bin. Such beauty in motion. Of course, organizing the activities and counting all those membership dollars would be a bother, but everyone makes sacrifices. And just think how we'd be improving the health and fitness of the average, stressed-out Modern Man.

I think I'll put an ad in the paper tomorrow: "Gold Mine Goat Health Club." (You bring the gold, I'll make it mine.) "Breathe in that fresh, country air while exercising your body." That's a spring ad. I'll have to change the wording slightly during breeding season.

Money, you understand, is not all that important to me. If it were, I wouldn't be raising goats. My *real* motive is to help the out-of-condition yuppies of the world improve their physical fitness -- while they, coincidentally, pay off my mortgage.

GOAT SWAPS

"Johnny, guess what?!" I bubbled to my spouse as he came through the door.

"Don't tell me -- you won the Publisher's Clearinghouse Sweepstakes!"

"No?"

"Then what?"

"I sold a goat!" Johnny, I knew, would be delighted, since he thinks we have about three times more goats than we need.

"I'd better sit down," he said and sat. "For how much?"

"Well, it's like this," I began... then unfolded one of my notorious goat deals. "You see, dear, I didn't really want to sell Thea, and I just couldn't ask what she's worth..."

"Why not?!" he interrupted. "You've certainly *paid* enough for goats."

"Now, Johnny, please listen. This is a good deal for both of us."

"Hmmph."

"She paid me $100 plus a doe kid back."

"Good grief, why do you want a doe kid back? I thought you were cutting down."

"I won't get her back until spring, when she's born, if she is. Otherwise, I'll have to wait another year."

"Well, thank goodness for that. What if Thea never has another doe?" he asked hopefully.

"I guess I'd take a buck."

He groaned. "That's just what we need, another buck. Then there'd be one buck for every doe -- a nice monogamous arrangement."

"Now, dear, you're exaggerating."

But he wasn't finished: "What if your buyer sells Thea before she kids?"

"She won't," I assured him.

"But what if she does?" he insisted.

"I might buy her back myself."

At this point Johnny buried his face in his hands. "Please, say no more," he begged. "I can't handle this much good news all at once."

Although my dear husband tends to overreact to my "deals", it does seem that more trading than selling goes on between me and other goat breeders. I've swapped oil paintings, potatoes, airplane rides, and restaurant meals for livestock. I've traded goats for sheep, goats for pigs, and goats for goats.

Three-way trades really get complicated. Once I let a buyer pay me off in farm-fresh eggs. However, I had plenty of eggs from my own chickens, so I traded the surplus to a third party for... no, not money... home-baked bread. Unfortunately, the bread deal ended when the baker moved out of town. I fattened the pigs that year on farm fresh eggs.

I'm still involved in a goat deal that started many years ago. A friend moved to Alaska and sold her doe to a mutual friend, with a doe kid back... someday. Friend #2 sold the doe to me, with the understanding that I owed the friend in Alaska a doe kid. I sold the doe, who was by then rather elderly, to someone else, assuring Alaska that she could have a kid out of my herd, closely related to her original doe, someday. Alaska is now living where she has no place for goats. I'll have to stay in the goat business just to settle this deal.

The all-time prize for a "goat deal" goes to two local boys who talked a neighbor out of twenty chickens with their sad story of parents out of work and very little food to eat. Those young entrepreneurs then tried to trade me twenty chickens for a wether goat which they wanted for a pet. The parents, it turned out, were not out of work and didn't want chickens OR a goat.

Nice try, though.

FEEDING FRIENDS

I take perverse pleasure in feeding goat meat and milk to unsuspecting people. Especially to those who have informed me that they can "smell goat milk a mile away." My father, as a small boy, had tasted his neighbor's goat milk, and the taste nearly made him retch. Yes, he'd agree, the goat's ill health and filthy environment might have had something to do with the taste, but still...

Dad reluctantly tasted our milk and said, "Well, it doesn't taste BAD, but it does taste like goat milk." So one day I challenged him to a taste test. One glass would contain cow's milk, the other goat's milk. My mother would keep us honest. Dad tasted glasses A and B -- and admitted that both were good, but B was definitely goat milk. Hah! B was cow milk! We won! From that day since, my father drinks our milk without comment.

Other people are tougher to win over. We invited friends for supper who raved about the ribs we served. "These are delicious!" We just smiled. "The best we've ever eaten!" We smiled some more. "What kind of meat is this, anyway?"

"Just something we raise," we smiled.

After dinner we confessed that the ribs were chevon. "I thought I detected an aftertaste," muttered the woman, who had done most of the raving. Some people could be fed cherry pie and enjoy it -- then get nauseous when told the cherries were really nanny berries.

But my fondest memories are of the couple who forewarned us: "We'd love to come over for a picnic. But *please* don't feed us goat meat or milk. We've had both before, and we just don't like the taste. Frankly, Linda, even the *thought* of it makes us ill."

"Thanks for letting us know. We'll have plenty of choices, don't worry," I assured her.

And we did -- they could choose between goat bologna, goat frankfurters, or goat cheese spread. They could drink goat milk shakes or coffee with goat cream. Our guests had some of everything, not realizing what they were eating -- and loved it all. Weeks later they stopped by again. I offered them lunch. "But I'm afraid all I have is this goat meat bologna for sandwiches," I apologized.

"Why, that looks just like the bologna we ate at your picnic."

"Oh, that's right!" I said with surprise. "I forgot you'd already tasted it. You liked it, as I recall. Good. Lunch will be ready in a jiffy."

What could they say?

I'm sure a good psychologist could explain why I like to torment people this way. Maybe I have a nasty desire to make people feel foolish. Or maybe I just have a healthy urge to cure people's unfounded food prejudices. Then again... it could be purely business-oriented behavior. Several people have asked to buy "yummy goat meat" after being tricked into eating it at our house. Whatever my innermost purpose, feeding unsuspecting friends goat meat and milk IS a good marketing strategy. Besides, it's fun.

FLYING GOATS

My goats are pretty good about staying where they belong -- most of the time. But when they do escape, they escape in a dramatic way. The whole herd may barge past me and a half-opened gate to reach the cherry tree beckoning from in front of the barn. To prevent damage from predatory goats, we crossfenced the fruit trees away from the barn. We have crossfences between crossfences with gates everywhere. If we placed all our gates side by side, they'd enclose a ten acre field.

When I say "gate", I'm using the term loosely. We do have some "real" gates, the metal or wood kind that swing; but most are what I call "Wyoming" gates. Woven wire attached to a post that fits into wire loops at the top and bottom of another post which is attached to the fence. Well, theoretically the gate post fits into the wire loops. Actually, once the gate is opened, the bottom of its post never again fits back in the loop. Not for me, anyway. Johnny has pulled the wire so tight it takes six men and a fence stretcher to close gates. So I don't open them. I climb over. So do the goats.

They must. I can think of no other way a goat can migrate from pasture A through pasture B into pasture C when no gates are open. And yet that happens regularly. Once a kid, Spirit, was hollering her head off from over by the lambing shed. The lambing shed is two fields and two five-foot woven-wire fences removed from where Spirit belonged. I could find no holes in the fences, no open gates, and Spirit could find no way to get back where she came from.

Even stranger was the episode with a kid one cool, autumn evening. As I headed for the barn, after dark, to do chores, I heard a kid baaing from what sounded like the middle of our pond. The middle of the pond? No, couldn't be. So I went about my chores.

All the while I milked, I heard what sounded like a kid goat, crying from what sounded like the middle of the pond. Finally I grabbed a flashlight and went to investigate. There, standing in the middle of the pond, was a goat, belly deep in water, shivering. She had found the underground peninsula that stretches most of the way across the upper end of the pond. From the looks of her, she'd been in much deeper water (the rest of the pond is six feet deep) and was afraid to move for fear of falling off the edge again.

I launched the canoe and gently herded her along "safe" ground to shore. After drying and putting her back with the other weanlings, two fences away, I went to close the gates I knew must be open. They weren't. In the morning, I examined fences for holes. There were none. I could see no way that kid could have gone from her pen to the pond. And why would she have fallen in anyhow? Kids are sure-footed and the pond bank is not steep. My son decided an alien had swooped down in a spaceship, picked her up to examine her, then set her back down -- in the water. "Well, how were they to know goats don't like to swim?"

I don't really believe that goat was abducted by a UFO, but I have no idea how she *did* get into the pond.

Even when I'm watching a goat escape, I sometimes don't believe my eyes. Like the time I put a doe into a buck pen surrounded by a six-foot high, solid board fence. The doe did not agree with me or the buck that she was in heat. She tore back and forth looking for a way out. As she charged into a corner and stopped with her shoulder against the fence, the buck snorted up from behind. She saw him coming and leaped upward -- clearing the 6 foot fence from a standstill. The buck blinked his eyes and turned this way and that looking for her. I didn't believe it either. But as I hurried around the side of the pen to see if she was hurt, I caught sight of her racing across the neighbor's field, a good quarter mile away. It took me an hour to catch her. That was Gerda, a grade Alpine, forever after known as Gerda the Gazelle.

I've never seen one of my Nubians leap a fence, nor have I seen them fly. But, somehow, one of them occasionally lands in a paddock several fences removed from the original. Apparently, the escapees don't know how they got where they are, either, since none have ever found their way back. They just run up and down the fence crying -- or stand in the water shivering, as the case may be. Either we have a resident flock of UFO's that like to play practical jokes, or my goats have an extraordinary ability to get *out* coupled with a total inability to reverse the procedure and get back *in*.

TANNING HIDES

One of the first -- and few -- things my husband liked about goats was their hides. He wanted to make a bedspread from the hides of wethers we butchered for meat. That was years ago. We still don't have that bedspread. (Thank goodness. I can't stand the thought of sleeping under dead goats.) But we do have numerous hides, both sheep and goat, stashed about the place, tanned by every method known to man, and a few more.

The first method we tried was acid tanning. Even though sulphuric acid made me nervous, I helped -- at first. When we transferred a sheep hide from the acid mix to a neutralizing mixture, my nervousness turned to terror. Bubbles hissed threateningly and suddenly up, over the top of the barrel, and cascaded across the lawn. Johnny agreed to try a different method.

Indian brain tanning seemed safer, until we learned that handling raw brains can transmit some dreadful disease -- I forget what. I think it's a parasitic disease that eats its way into the goat or human brain, gobbling up gray matter, little by little.

Neither of us felt we had any gray matter to spare, so we settled on the alum tan. About this time, I turned the project over to Johnny. The acid experience had unnerved me -- besides, I hate scraping hides.

Although alum does not produce as soft a finished product as brain tanning or the commercial process, it's good enough for rugs, seat covers -- and probably bedspreads. (Commercial tanners cheat by splitting the layers of skin.) After much practice, Johnny has grown proficient at producing medium-soft hair-on hides. With one notable exception.

Quite a number of years ago, I purchased a beautiful, spotted, purebred Nubian doe. She cost plenty, but she was worth it -- or would have been if she hadn't died of tetanus two weeks later. Of course, I spent a fortune in vet bills trying to save her. Johnny was determined to keep her hide; he wanted to have something to show for all that money. And show it he does, to everyone who comes around.

"Look at this one," he exhorts visitors. "This is the most expensive goat hide in the world." It's also the stiffest. The hide turned out as rigid as the goat was when she died.

Johnny has written his own how-to sheet on tanning, but I have to laugh when I read it. The directions are deceptively simple. "Using a hog scraper, remove the flesh from the hide." When people ask how long this step takes, Johnny answers truthfully, "I can scrape a full-grown goat hide in thirty minutes." The poor, deluded people wonder what they're doing wrong when, three hours of hard labor later, they've only exposed one small piece of skin. I should add to Johnny's instructions: "Wife's best time is three days and at least fifty sore muscles."

Of course, at the end of three days, the hide has rotted. That's another thing instructions don't tell -- how long a hide will keep without salting or drying. Not long enough. Every hide we've waited to salt because "salt rusts the scraper and I'll get to it tomorrow" has decomposed in forty-eight hours -- with the help of instant-hatching maggots. Flies love goat hides. In fact, the quickest way to take the hair off a hide is leave it in the sun -- out of the reach of dogs. (Dogs love hides, too.) Maggots eat the rotting flesh; ergo, the hair falls out. Unfortunately, the skin is then too tender to tan. (Filet mignon, according to Johnny, is flesh in the early stages of rot. I wouldn't eat filet mignon if you paid me.)

Johnny's tanning instructions suggest cleansing the scraped hide in a washing machine on the gentle cycle. I would suggest only doing that in your neighbor's machine when he's gone on vacation (if you hate your neighbor) or in your own machine if you're looking for an excuse to buy a new one. Few things are more revolting than bits of goat flesh stuck to your underwear -- or whatever is in the next load.

Actually, I would suggest tanning hides only if you or your spouse have biceps the size of basketballs, plenty of spare time... and an extra washing machine.

DASHED DREAMS

"Don't count your chickens before they hatch" has always been one of my mother's favorite expressions. I never fully absorbed this advice until I had goats, not chickens.

For a very long time, I had dreamed of artificially inseminating one of my does to a truly outstanding, but long dead buck -- a buck whose semen was way out of my price range. Then the price came down. I bought two straws. Ellie, bless her heart, came back in heat seven days after I used the first straw, so she got both. I waited eagerly for her to kid -- absolutely sure that my investment would produce a grand champion, Top Ten doe.

The day finally arrived. Ellie, who always kids quickly and effortlessly, fooled around for hours. Unable to stand the suspense, I scrubbed up and went inside. Something wet, warm and soft -- very soft -- met my groping fingers. I won't go into the rest of the grisly details, but the baby Ellie and I finally delivered was grossly deformed, with its insides not enclosed within the body cavity, as insides ought to be. Especially the insides of a grand champion, Top Ten doe.

Oh, well, there were more kids in there, and Ellie rapidly shot them out. Just as rapidly I wiped their noses free of mucus and upended them to check the sex. Surely, one must be a doe.

They were both bucks. Beautiful bucks, though. Too bad one of them had four teats. Far from being a grand champion, a four-teated buck can't even be registered. He was destined to be raised for meat by Mexican friends who say goats taste the same no matter how much their daddy's semen cost and no matter how many teats they have.

The other was a handsome red and white spotted fellow with long, white ears -- the sole heir to my dreams. As an only child, Epic grew quickly, nursing from his milky mother, playing in the goat yard with the other kids. Their favorite resting spot was under the manure spreader, as it has been for many generations of goats.

Each time we use the spreader and return it, we prop the tongue on a cement block. For some reason, one day we apparently left the tongue standing on its own retractable foot, instead of on the cement block. I never noticed the difference until my husband ran into the house one night, greatly agitated. "Hurry, everybody! I need help! The manure spreader fell on a goat!"

Terrified, I dashed to the barn. My vision of a prized milking doe splattered all over the ground was, fortunately, inaccurate. However, the tongue had caught one of Epic's forelegs, and he stood crying, trying to escape. We lifted the tongue, and Epic hobbled to his mom on three legs -- the fourth hanging useless, broken just above the fetlock.

For two months, my grand-champion-doe-turned-buck lived in a separate pen with his mother and a full leg cast. Which was a lucky thing. Because that meant he was not with the other baby goats on test day -- the day I forgot to latch the kid pen and all of the little monsters escaped and nursed their dams. Only Ellie still had milk when the tester arrived. So much for any Top Ten records in the making. (Ellie is a good milker, but not that good.)

I'm not the only goat breeder with dashed dreams. A friend wrote one spring to tell me how excited she was about the doe she'd A-I'd to my proven, deceased, buck, Hondo. The doe looked huge -- much bigger than when she gave birth to twins. My friend was sure of triplets, maybe even quads. Not unlikely, I told her, because another breeder had reported quads from that semen -- three bucks and a doe.

The next letter I received was not so jubilant. The goat kidded -- with one buck. A nice, big buck, to be sure, but a buck -- not a grand champion, Top Ten doe with two or three lovely siblings.

Goats are sneaky about what they're carrying. In March, one of my goats looked like she was pregnant with quads -- even though she'd aborted in January. Another goat I didn't think was bred had twins. I know now why she didn't look pregnant: she has no body. When she was carrying kids, she looked like a normal goat. Now she's an udder with four legs and a head.

Ah, but each breeding season brings out the optimist in me. Until I find out differently, I'll pretend that a whole herd of grand champion, Top Ten does will be born on my farm next spring. I just won't count them.

THE-TWO-WEEKS-
BETWEEN-THE-END-
OF-BREEDING-SEASON-
AND-THE-BEGINNING-
OF-KIDDING-SEASON

HAIRY BLIMPS

I hate it when people come to look at my goats in December. People expect beautiful, sleek, dairy goats. What they see are big, hairy blimps.

"When is this goat expecting kids? Tomorrow? She's huge!"

"Uh, no. I just bred her yesterday."

"Really? She's so *fat*."

My goats are not really fat. They're just ready for winter. All that hair makes them *look* fat. Or so I try to convince my customers.

Most December goat shoppers are looking for cute little Christmas presents. My kids are not cute, little frolicking babies anymore. They're big, hairy, almost-yearlings -- with sharp hoofs that like to beat muddy tattoos on visitors' chests.

"Do you have anything a little smaller?" gasps a potential customer, cowering in the corner while four eager heads nibble on her coat sleeves, boot tops, hair and fingers.

"How about a kitten?" I suggest.

Other December goat-lookers are just getting into goats and want to start with quality animals. I try to keep them in the house looking at pedigrees and show records and drinking tea. If they haven't put down a deposit before we get to the barn, all is lost. I'll never convince them that the fat, hairy ox standing on their foot is a permanent champion with a gorgeous udder. I find it hard to believe myself.

Maybe we Northerners should take videos of our animals during the spring and summer months, when they're flush with milk and beautiful. I could show movies to a customer in my heated home while the cold wind whistles outdoors. Once he made his selection, I'd blindfold him, load his newly-purchased goat into his truck, and only remove the blindfold after he was behind the wheel and ready to drive off.

"Now, remember," I'd admonish the buyer. "Keep your eyes closed until she kids next March."

I wouldn't mind if other long-time goat breeders came by in December. Their goats look just like mine. However, goat breeders never tour my barn in the wintertime. They don't need to look at big, hairy blimps. They have enough of their own.

Some December visitors arrive with a goat in tow to be bred. They want to see the daughters of the buck they're using for service. Unfortunately, his daughters are just as big, fat and hairy as their doe. "What will he improve?" they ask dubiously. That's the signal to go back in the house and look at pedigrees, show and milk records. Those are much more impressive than the hooved mounds of hair and blubber in my barn.

Perhaps goat breeders in southern climes don't have these problems. I wouldn't mind going south one of these winters to find out. I'd probably be so awestruck I'd bring back a carload of sleek, slender goats -- goats who would quickly turn fat and hairy -- or get pneumonia and die.

No, there's no escaping a northern winter. Videos are the best plan. Ski shops have videos of skiers flying gracefully down scenic, snowy slopes. Windsurfing shops have videos of sailboarders, leaning joyously into the wind, doing intricate maneuvers around buoys. I could have videos of my impeccably-groomed does, walking proudly and sedately around show rings, looking sleek and beautifully-uddered, winning rosettes. My customer would be so mesmerized he wouldn't even notice the fat, hairy blob standing on his foot, nibbling the buttons on his coat. Or he wouldn't until he arrived home with the blimp instead of the vision he saw on my video screen.

Buying a goat in December takes a lot of faith.

FIFTY DOLLAR
SODA FOUNTAINS

In December, my phone starts to ring with people eager to buy goats.

"Do you have a nanny for sale? I want one that milks at least a gallon a day."

"In December?" I ask dubiously, then try to explain that my goats freshened last spring, are now rebred and at their lowest level of production -- if not already dry. The caller, however, isn't interested in lactation curves for dairy goats. All he wants is a goat giving lots of milk -- now.

"Sorry, I haven't any does still milking a gallon," I tell the insistent caller. "If I did, they wouldn't be for sale. I have a two-year-old due in February I'd sell for $150."

"A HUNDRED FIFTY DOLLARS FOR A GOAT??!!" explodes the caller. "I bought the last one for thirty-five at the auction!"

"How much milk did she give?"

"Close to two gallons when we got her."

Auction goats give a lot of milk at first because they haven't been milked for two days. Then they mysteriously dry up. Although the reasons are not really mysterious. I was a nursing mother. I know what would have happened to *me* if I'd gone two days without nursing -- then been hauled to the auction block.

But I'm not convinced many auction goats give two gallons even the first day. Some people use imagination, not a dairy scale, to measure their milk. Two gallons is composed of 3 quarts milk, 1 quart foam and 4 quarts wishful thinking.

One lady called looking for goats that milked "an honest" two gallons a day... and she was willing to pay up to $50 apiece for them. I told her to let me know if she found more than she needed -- I'm always in the market for $50 goats that milk two gallons in December. I haven't heard from her yet.

Why can't folks who want heavy milkers call in the spring, when I have them? (Although not for $50.) In the spring, everyone wants brush goats.

"I have five acres of blackberries," my neighbor informs me. "I won't charge you a thing if you bring your nannies over here and stake them out to eat." I thank him for his generosity and politely decline, explaining that dairy goats eat good quality hay and grain (and expensive rose bushes, if they get a chance), sleep in barns and are not tied where their udders can get scratched or they can be harassed by dogs or strangle themselves. And while angora goats and brush goats are often called nannies and billies, dairy goats are *does* and *bucks*. By the sixth such call, I'm not polite anymore. "NO! NO! A THOUSAND TIMES NO!"

In December, along with people looking for heavy milkers are parents looking for Christmas presents for their kids. "Baby goats are *so* cute," gushes a mother as she looks over my December-born kids. "I'd like to give our son a baby goat for Christmas."

"For a 4-H project?" I inquire, hoping she's talking about a different son than the toddler I just retrieved from the pregnant yearling pen, where he was trying to unscrew Nubian ears from Nubian heads.

"Oh, dear, no," she laughs. "Our little boy just turned three. I just want a goat for him to play with."

"How about a stuffed toy goat instead?" I suggest. "It won't mind being dragged around by the tail or left out in the rain."

"But a stuffed toy can't love him back," she protests.

I feel like telling her that she's presuming a lot if she thinks a baby goat will love a creature that pulls its ears. But I don't. Instead I explain that baby goats cannot be treated like toys, must be fed twice a day, every day, not just on Christmas, and will cry if left alone, so really need to live in pairs. Besides, baby goats grow up (if they're lucky) and aren't quite so cute when they weigh 200 pounds.

"By the way, do you have a barn?" I ask her.

"No, but we could make a little bed in the garage." I think the lady has puppies and goats confused.

I also get a lot of calls from folks who acquired goats in the spring and want to know why their doe isn't milking yet. "She's almost a year old. When will she give milk?"

"Five months after she's bred," I respond.

"Oh."

Non-farm raised adults don't realize goats must produce kids before they'll produce milk. Many also don't know that their goat must be milked twice a day, rain or shine. Some folks think goats operate like soda fountains. You milk them when you're thirsty or ready to make a pumpkin pie.

I'm happy to educate callers about dairy goats, but I wonder if I'm making any progress. Just as many people as ever call wanting two gallon milkers in December. Maybe I'm the one who needs education.

Maybe that lady *will* call back with a line on a herd of $50 supermilkers, and I can buy some, too. Goats that good probably *don't* need to be bred to produce milk. They're just soda fountains with ears. I'll milk when I'm thirsty and pull the covers back over my head if the weather's cold and snowy.

Lady, if you've found those goats, please call me collect.

DEAR SANTA

Every year just before Christmas, the members of my family sit down, adjust their individual halos, and write their letters to Santa Claus. Since we give each other mainly home-made gifts (like bumpy hand-knit hats), and gifts of service (like certificates for "one load of firewood, hauled without complaining"), we depend on Santa for any materialistic desires we may harbor. Some of our requests sound outlandish, but what could be too difficult for a guy who covers the entire world in one night with just a sleigh and eight tiny reindeer for transportation?

Here is one of my letters.

Dear Santa,

How are you and Mrs. Claus this year, Santa? Jolly as ever, I trust. Ho Ho Ho. I just love people who laugh as easily as you do, Santa. This world could use more laughter, don't you agree?

As always, I've been incredibly good. Now is not the time for your "Ho Ho Ho", Santa. I'm being serious. Just listen to this -- I actually sold goats for *cash* this year, instead of for future offspring. I hardly think taking back a doe I sold as a kid five years ago counts. Her owner moved to town and wanted a good home for her. This must be a good home, else why do so many goats that leave here come back?

Better still, I did not write even one scathing letter to the bureaucracy that runs the dairy goat registry.

However, after hearing how much it will cost me to get the annual production, show, and classification summaries, I'm sorely tempted. So my first request is for those books, dear Santa. You will probably be swamped with this same request from other less-than-wealthy goat breeders. I don't know if they're all deserving, but those goat breeders who read and enjoy my column in United Caprine News are definitely the right sort. I humbly ask you to grant their requests.

Speaking of humility, I've made giant strides in that department -- thanks to my does and the semen tank. After successfully breeding one doe A-I last year, I threw myself into the project with high hopes this fall. My technique is definitely improving: I haven't scalded any semen yet, unlike last year. But my timing is still off. Nonetheless, by next breeding season, I'll be ready to A-I all these superior doelings I'm creating. (Anything that takes four straws of semen to create must be superior.)

And that, Santa, brings me to my next request. My supergoats-to-be deserve the best. Unfortunately, the mates I have in mind for them have pretty spendy semen, like $100 per straw. Believe me, I would never dare to ask for this if I hadn't been so remarkably good all year. (There you go again with that "Ho Ho Ho", Santa. Sometimes your timing is a bit off, too, you know.) Luckily, the more straws a person buys, the cheaper it is. Why, I can get five straws of a really terrific buck's semen for a mere $400. That's like getting one straw free! Such a bargain.

That's all I need this year, Santa. I know it isn't much, but I never have been greedy. (I'm beginning to wish you'd choke on your "Ho's", Santa.)

Goodness, did I forget to thank you for the stuff you left last Christmas? I'm terribly sorry. Your little gifts were really something. I think I understand why you didn't leave the stock trailer I requested -- it was those smoking letters I wrote while serving on the American Dairy Goat Association Official Testing committee, wasn't it? Well, you can be sure I behaved myself this year. Anyhow, it was no problem stuffing five 4-H'ers and their goats in the back seat of my compact car. After all, we were only going a hundred and thirty miles.

And I really did appreciate the left-handed hoof trimmers, even though I'm right-handed. If I break my right arm tomorrow, I won't have a thing to worry about, all because of your thoughtfulness. Yes, sir, your gifts really hit the spot, Santa.

The best of everything to you and Mrs. Claus. Give my love to the elves.

Your grateful friend,

Linda Fink

p.s. One last item. I could really use a glass case for all the Grand Champion ribbons and trophies my supergoats-to-be will win.

CHRISTMAS DAY

When the kids were young, we always loaded the family in the car and went to my folks' place for Christmas. Mom fixed a sumptuous meal of turkey and dressing, mashed potatoes and gravy, candied sweet potatoes, cranberry sauce (two kinds), black olives, carrot and celery sticks, Mom's Fancy Molded Salad, and pies, lots of them -- apple and pumpkin and mincemeat and walnut. Traditionally, dinner was served at 2 p.m. Unfortunately, every year we were late. That became traditional, too.

We tried so hard to get there on time. All the gifts were packed the night before, along with sleeping bags for the ride home, cameras, and lots of et cetera. We opened our own gifts early Christmas morning, then dashed about doing chores. Theoretically, we were ready to leave by 11 a.m. Mom and Dad live just two hours away. We should have had plenty of time.

However, between theory and reality lay thirty-some goats, each with his or her own technique for delaying our departure. Being a democratic group, they took turns.

One year Deedee got sick on Christmas Day -- so sick we had to call our poor vet, who wished he'd gone into a less demanding profession. My mom wished our goats would either stay well or die quickly; the turkey was getting cold.

Another year the bucks conspired to break down fences and breed every doe left to breed. My husband was hammering boards back together, muttering under his breath about those blankety-blank, stinkin', trouble-makin' bucks, while I was on the phone: "Mom, I'm afraid we'll be late... the bucks got out." I heard a sigh through the receiver.

Or someone would turn up missing. "All 12 yearlings were here last night, I KNOW they were. Someone must have stolen Jabberwocky," I lamented tearfully.

"Bah," said my husband. "Who'd want that loud-mouth? She's here somewhere."

Sure enough, she'd managed to stuff her pregnant belly through the holes in the manger and was nestled comfortably in the hay. Getting her out again required six stout men, all of whom had better things to do on Christmas morning.

Then there was the doe who went into labor two weeks early.

"I can't leave, yet, dear; her kids will be small, coming so early. I'll have to feed them and get them dry quickly."

My husband paced the floor waiting for goat kids more than he ever did for our own. And he was forever checking his watch. "Can't you make her hurry? We're an hour late already!" But a doe who usually delivers kids before you can get her to the kidding pen, takes forever on Christmas Day.

"We invited you for Christmas, not New Year's," chided my mother, when we finally arrived. But she melted when we showed her the newborns we brought along. So what if dinner was at 10 p.m. and the children fell asleep before opening the gifts their grandparents so lovingly selected?

However, even the most forgiving mother has her limits. One year, my mom reached hers.

"This Christmas," my long-suffering mother said, "Why don't we come to YOUR house."

"Sure Mom, we'd love to have you over here. Dinner's at 2 p.m.," I confidently announced, secretly wondering how I could get a turkey cooked and everything else done.

"Linda," sighed my mother, "I'll bring the food. All you have to do is set the table and BE there."

I didn't tell her I was waiting anxiously for my prize doe to come in heat, so I could take her to that fantastic buck forty miles away... Surely that wouldn't happen on Christmas Day... would it?

NEW YEAR'S RESOLUTIONS

Whenever I make New Years resolutions, I feel defeated and guilty if I can't keep them. Defeated and guilty is a miserable way to feel. And when I'm miserable, so is everyone around me.

Therefore, in the sincere desire to keep everyone (most of all, myself) happy, I do hereby solemnly resolve to make no foolish promises about: cutting down my herd size, keeping the barn clean, trimming hooves regularly, keeping up on vaccinations, or milking within sixteen hours of the previous milking.

I further resolve to stop nagging myself about leaving for shows on time. That's my husband's job; I shouldn't usurp his responsibility. What better way to get the adrenaline flowing than to leave at 7 a.m. for a goat show that starts at 8 a.m. -- one hundred miles away. I've been doing it for years.

Psychiatrists say many of us become depressed because we set unrealistic goals for ourselves. Therefore, I resolve to stop expecting much of anything from myself or my goats. If my goats don't make Top Ten, I solemnly resolve not to slit my wrists. If they don't win Grand Championships, I resolve not to slit the judge's wrists...but I reserve the right to mutter under my breath. However, if my goats don't earn their "stars"... I'll cry. A star is given for a mere 1500 pounds of milk. And there's nothing unrealistic about a goat averaging 5 pounds a day for 300 days.

In past years, I resolved to keep my mouth shut when disagreements arose. My mouth, unfortunately, has an opinion on everything and never cooperated with my resolve. I hereby resolve to stop feeling guilty about the excesses of my mouth.

My goats would prefer I write a different set of resolutions. They're not at all interested in the petty squabbles I become embroiled in; they have their own pecking order to fight over. But I'm sure they'd like me to resolve to buy them prime alfalfa instead of long-past-its-prime grass hay, even if I must sell my right arm to do so (as long as I become proficient milking with just one hand).

My goats would also like an increased grain ration, better working conditions, shorter work year (lactation), less overtime (weekend shows), and better job security (no culling).

If Johnny made resolutions for me they'd be: feed less grain, cut back on hay, sell, sell, and sell. I can hear them all screaming at me now:

Goats: "Tenure!"

Johnny: "Sell!"

Goats: "Retirement benefits!"

Johnny: "Cull!"

To keep from becoming schizophrenic, I'll make my own resolutions -- guaranteed to please no one but me. My non-resolutions will relieve rather than increase my feelings of guilt and anxiety.

No more silly vows to climb out of bed every hour to A-I a doe the moment she goes out of heat (the best time). I always turn the alarm off and fall right back to sleep. Why brow-beat myself for doing what comes naturally?

No more useless agreements with my spouse to "sell down". We both know if I sell one goat, I'll keep four kids to replace her. Why be ashamed of succumbing to the inevitable?

No more kicking myself with phrases like: "I should clean the barn; I ought to trim hooves; I must clip udders." Those chores have waited a long time; what's another month?

This year, as I erase the "shoulds", "oughts" and "musts" from my life, I anticipate a new sense of self-acceptance and self-worth...

And a dirtier barn.

FASCINATING CHARACTERS

Invariably, non-goat-owning visitors, and we have plenty, remark on how personable our goats are. "They're like people, aren't they?" gushes a city woman, who has been exclaiming loudly and continuously about everything since her arrival three hours earlier.

"Better than people," I tell her. "Goats don't talk."

Goats do know how to communicate their feelings. But some of them, like some people, have personalities that clash with mine.

Thuja was one of those. She was raised on her mother, but that's no excuse. I've had other momma-raised milkers who didn't flee in terror at my approach. I swear I never mistreated her. She was just a natural born squirrel-brain.

Thuja, the squirrel brain, darted into the milk room and charged around the milkstand three or four times before soaring onto it. Then she gulped down her food as though it was her first meal in a week. She cowered when I approached with the bucket and trembled while I milked. As soon as I finished, she resumed her frantic dancing in place until I turned her loose. Then she flew out the door, knocking down anything and anyone in her path. Thuja was nuts.

Deedee has always been just the opposite. She loves everyone. People were created, Deedee is convinced, to scratch goat backs and say sweet things in goat ears.

Every visitor is greeted warmly by this queen of the herd. Deedee lifts her muzzle and looks soulfully into the new human's eyes, then rubs her head lovingly on his or her torso. But woe be to the foolish goat who tries to share the attention. Deedee knocks the competitor senseless -- then returns serenely to her human for more petting. Dozens of people have said to me, "This goat really likes me. She hasn't left my side since I came in here." None of them suspect that Deedee is shamefully fickle. Tomorrow, she'll be loving up someone else.

Deedee's sister Delilah is just as loving, but not so ostentatious about it. She stands quietly by my side, closing her eyes in pleasure while I scratch her, but not trying to crawl into my pocket when I don't. She doesn't vie for attention from visitors, because her twin Deedee always gets there first.

Visitors know Delilah best as The Sitting Goat. She rests on her haunches like a dog. Many family vacation albums have a picture of the strange sitting goat of Fink Family Farm. Delilah first found that position comfortable when she was three years old and hugely pregnant with five big kids. Her belly was so enormous that lying down was impossible. Resting her weight on her tailbone seemed the best solution. At the age of thirteen, she still prefers sitting on her tailbone.

A somewhat younger member of the herd, Ellie is a very ordinary goat... in most ways. She's friendly, but not overly so, and she lies down normally. However, Ellie does have one personality quirk: she cleans her teeth. At least, I think that's what she's doing. The does' heads are secured on the milkstand with chains across the keyholes. The excess chain hangs down on the head side of the board. When Ellie is through eating grain, she grabs the chain in her mouth and scrapes her teeth along it several times -- for all the world like she's flossing the grain out of her teeth. Ellie will not leave the milkstand until she has completed this piece of personal hygiene.

And then there's Total Eclipse. Total specializes in injuries -- both to herself and others. I don't think she has ever accepted her status as a goat. In younger days, Total had dreams, I'm sure, of being a daredevil motorcyclist, riding in circles on steep, curved walls before a spell-bound audience. Whenever visitors came, she sped around the barn, bouncing off vertical walls and doing intricate airborne maneuvers. Then she pranced up to the guest and baaa'ed expectantly, as if waiting for the applause.

When she was four, Total fractured a leg performing tricks and spent show season in a cast. The next year she stayed on the ground long enough to earn glory in the showring, even though she did those same airborne feats whenever a milkout was called.

Now old and plump, Total is too big to get off the ground, so she spends her time teaching tricks to younger does -- whether they want to learn or not. A well-aimed toss of Total's massive head sends doelings flying across the barn. Kids quickly learn how to land feet first on a wall and ricochet off, just as Total used to do. She's a dedicated instructor.

I wonder why goats have the personalities they have. Some traits must be hereditary and others environmental, but neither explains Theo. Theo was one of the sweetest, friendliest kids ever raised on this farm -- even though she was raised by Thuja the squirrel-brain. Either the personality Theo inherited skipped a generation, or Thuja was dropped on her head at birth.

Maybe I was dropped on my head, too, to spend so much time in a goat barn. Some members of my family think so. But goats are personable creatures, as every visitor soon learns. The real mystery is how, having come to know goats as personalities, anyone can resist owning a hundred of the fascinating creatures? And why are such resisters always married to goat lovers?

"Because," responded my husband when I asked him that question, "anyone who marries a goat lover already has one strange but fascinating character to cope with -- his spouse. We don't need a hundred more."

A BAD, BAD DAY

Some days everything goes wrong. I remember one of those days. It started when I went out to milk and slipped on a frosty placenta I'd thrown out of the kidding pen about midnight. After picking myself and the milk pail off the ground, I limped into the milk parlor and turned on the water, only to find the pipes frozen. Then I remembered that, the day before, I'd unplugged the heat tape after using its socket for the disbudding iron. After burning the horn buds off baby goats, I'd forgotten to replug the heat tape.

I trudged back to the house for a kettle of hot water to thaw the pipes. The phone rang -- three calls before I could escape. When I finally returned, a flood of water was pouring out from under the milk room door. The pipes had thawed during my absence, but the drain under the sink had not. So water filled the sink, overflowing onto the floor. I rushed to turn off the spigot, only to slip and land on the icy floor -- *some* of the water was not flowing -- it was freezing to the concrete. Wet, cold, bruised, and fast losing my sense of humor, I cleaned up the mess, thawed the drain and went to the house to change clothes.

By that time, the goats were clamoring with impatience. They were also nervous about entering the milkroom after all the unusual commotion, and fidgety once on the stand. One of them stepped in the bucket. Rather than reassure her in a soothing voice, I practiced primal scream therapy, which left the terrified doe beating a tattoo in the bucket while milk danced all over me, her and the milkroom. The day was not starting well.

I bumbled through the rest of my chores without too many problems, cracking my head only once on the roof I always forget is low and being stepped on no more than half a dozen times by the ravenous yearlings as I filled their grain trough. Things were looking up.

I decided to rearrange the semen tank to make way for a bulk pack of semen arriving soon. A mistake. Oh, things went well enough at first. I transferred a few single straws into another cane successfully. Then I pulled the last cane out of the canister that would receive the bulk pack and tried to shove the cane into an almost full canister. It wouldn't go down. I jiggled and wiggled and pried and jostled, but it steadfastly refused to join the others. I couldn't leave it out in the "warm" air any longer, so I gave one final push on the obstinate cane. It slid alongside and down -- into the depths of the nitrogen tank. There it stayed, because, at that time I didn't have a tool to retrieve lost canes. Just as well, considering my mood. Irritable impatience is not the best frame of mind to be in when poking through semen tanks.

Nerves frayed, I grabbed a pitchfork and started cleaning pens. Hard physical labor always calms me. I forked my way vigorously through several small pens and moved on to one occupied by two young bucks. The bucks, feeling frisky in the cool air, cavorted down the aisle instead of into the pen I had ready for them. Oh well, the gate at the other end was closed. They could play in the aisle until I finished. Each time I took a wheelbarrow load to the garden, I carefully closed the aisle gate behind me. The bucks paid no attention. They were busy flirting with does across the fence.

The rhythmic work of forking manure eased my tension. All that remained was the loose hay under the manger. I gathered most of it into my arms and loaded it on the wheelbarrow. Then I took the pitchfork and leaned down to angle it into the packed hay that was left. I jabbed -- hard.

POP! POP! POP! POP! POP!

The rapid-fire explosions made me jump -- but not far enough or fast enough. The tines of my pitchfork had exploded a nest of rotten eggs. Gooey pieces of nauseating gunk rained down on me. I gagged, dropped the fork and ran for the house, wiping rotten slime from eyes and face as I went. Shedding my clothes on the back porch, I fled to the shower and turned the water on full force. After scrubbing all the garbage out of my hair, I let the warm water massage my battered body for a long time. I didn't want to face the rest of the day.

After awhile, the bathroom door opened and my husband's voice penetrated my sanctuary: "Linda? Are you in there?"

"Yeah, what about it?" I growled. He'd better not give me a hard time for showering in the middle of the day, I thought.

"Did you know two bucks were out -- pruning the orchard?"

I flew from the tub nude, and down the hall to grab clothes. My husband yelled after me: "Relax. We put them back." Then, apparently speaking to someone else, he said: "The bathroom's free now, if you want to wash up."

I froze where I stood in the bedroom, holding my breath and listening. A male voice I didn't recognize said: "I'd sure like to know what you said to make her move that fast. I'd like to try it on *my* wife." Chuckle chuckle.

My husband, laughing: "Oh, I just told her the goats were out. That's like yelling "Fire!" around here."

More laughter.

Then my husband's voice again: "Thanks for the ride home. I'll get Linda to take me back to the truck with some tools. The only thing I can count on that truck to do is break down.

"And thanks for helping catch the critters and put them away."

"No problem," replied The Male Voice. "It's always interesting going to someone's place the first time. You never know what you might see. Chuckle chuckle."

Mortified, I crawled into bed and pulled the covers up over my head. No one should have to endure a day like that. And it was only noon.

WARM FUZZIES

Goats may create problems, but, afterwards, they are the first to console us. They make wonderful friends. They're always interested in what you're doing. No goat would ever hide behind a newspaper and refuse to talk to you. She'd eat the newspaper and then nuzzle your face.

Unlike spouses, goats always notice when you wear a new coat. They react by leaping straight up in the air, dashing to the far side of the barn and standing, quivering. (A spouse might react in a similar fashion, but only after hearing the price.)

Not until you take off your coat do goats believe you are the same person who fed them last night. Then they will deign to nibble the unfamiliar garment, pull it onto the straw and manure strewn floor, and step on it a few times. From then on, the coat is accepted. No matter what the price.

It's possible to be surrounded by people and still be lonely. It's not possible to be surrounded by goats and stay lonely for long. Goats won't allow it. They'll pester you until you acknowledge their presence by scratching their necks or talking to them. If you start daydreaming and stop scratching, they are apt to give you a little nip to wake you up again. Goats believe in living in the here and now. Here is my back -- now scratch it.

Whether you're working or relaxing, goats will do it with you. They'll chew on the hammer, stand on the board you're trying to lift, or climb into your lap. Goats will not ignore you.

People, say psychologists, need warm fuzzies -- things that make us feel good. Like being gently touched. People, then, should keep goats. Goats love to touch. A doe's soft lips will touch your chin, gently caress your nose, all the while she's murmuring sweet nothings in your ear. And standing on your foot.

Goats love to give massages. They rub your legs... your back... anything they can lean against. In return, they ask only for room and board... and your undivided attention. At least Nubians do, and I raise Nubians.

Sometimes, the attention my goats lavish on me can cause minor problems. For example, once I decided to make myself beautiful by applying a comfrey facial. I washed a few comfrey leaves and stuffed them into the blender. Then I smeared the green paste all over my face.

Before the time arrived to wash off the hardened mask, it was time to feed baby goats. (That was back in the days when I was still bottle-feeding my kids, instead of momma-rearing them.) The kids were fascinated by the green stuff on my face. After sniffing it, they recognized the delicious smell of comfrey (delicious to a goat), and licked off my beauty mask. That is why I am not yet beautiful. But the goats don't care.

Which is another thing that makes goats such wonderful friends. They accept us with all our faults. If I am occasionally grumpy, that's okay. My does just stomp extra hard on my toes as they walk by, then turn and give me a forgiving rub on the backside.

Goats don't care if you're fat or skinny, cute or homely, graceful or clumsy. If you are the one who feeds and loves them, you're wonderful.

You're wonderful even if you say outrageous things that you couldn't say to your best human friend. Goats don't react with shock at anything you tell them. They just gaze soulfully into your eyes and nibble your collar. Have a problem? Tell it to a goat. She'll listen intently, give you a few encouraging nuzzles, and never betray your confidence. Even if you sell her to the person you were talking about.

Goat lovers should tell the world about goat friendships. We could start an advertising campaign. "Need a friend? Buy a goat. Instant companionship. Just add food, water and love." We could place folders extolling the virtues of goats in the offices of divorce lawyers.

"Does your spouse ignore you? Not understand you? Get a goat. Guaranteed love and acceptance. And no barking!"

"Tired of starting every morning facing the back page of the daily newspaper? Buy a goat. Start your days with love, warm breath, and fresh milk."

"Goats -- The Ultimate in Warm Fuzzies."

CRS

At a dairy goat convention I once attended, one of the speakers was a veterinarian from Washington State University. Along with the usual discussion of CAE, enterotoxemia, and mastitis, he described a disease called CRS. CRS is not a disease of goats, but rather of people. That vet first heard about it when his wife informed him that she had it. After he described his wife's symptoms, I was certain that I, too, am a victim.

CRS is characterized by an inability to remember simple things, such as which goats you just dewormed and which ones you didn't. I can't even remember which goats I've fed grain to and which ones I haven't. Lisbeth, a pregnant yearling, took advantage of my affliction to jump on the milkstand several times each day for her grain. At least, I suspect she did. I could never remember if I saw her up there a few minutes ago, or the day before. (Time tends to run together for CRS sufferers.)

One morning, in an attempt to catch Lisbeth in the act, I cleverly put a collar on her before turning her back into the barn. Normally, my goats live collarless. Sure enough, a few goats later, there she was again -- with collar, waiting impatiently for grain. I threw her out. Lisbeth screamed indignantly the rest of the time I was doing chores. I guess she thought she was "supposed" to come in time after time. The next day, she came in with the collar, so I took it off. When a collarless Lisbeth tried to bull her way into the milkroom, I stopped her. But that was the last day the scheme worked, because I could never remember whether it was a collar-on or collar-off day.

I also have trouble remembering which goats I've milked. Since I let kids nurse, the udders don't give much clue... except for slimy teats. If the teats are slimy, I haven't washed the udder preparatory to milking. Unfortunately, I've been known to wash an udder, then turn the goat back out without milking her.

I used to think I was just absent-minded. Indeed, my mind is often absent from the work at hand. Usually, it's in the show ring, at the head of the line, while the rest of me is home in the barn, shoveling manure or trimming hooves. It's rather comforting to know my affliction has a name. If they didn't know about CRS, goat breeder friends might think I was just dumb.

One winter an incident occurred which demonstrates how devastating this disease can be. I could not catch Ilsa, one of my prime show does, in heat. Daily, all through December and January, I took her for a walk down the buck aisle. To no avail. She just wasn't interested. In February, Ilsa started drying up. I went all through my calendar and at no time did any bucks get loose. "Why is Ilsa going down in her milk?" I agonized. "She couldn't be bred."

Then one late February day, I paged through the calendar one more time. There, on November 6th, plain as could be, were the words, "Ilsa in heat and bred to Epic." Where was my brain that November day? Certainly not home, paying attention to business.

Ilsa grew fat and happy. Happy that I was no longer peeking under her tail twice a day for signs of heat and dragging her down buck row.

After learning about CRS, I described the malady in a weekly column I write for a local newspaper. Lo and behold, a Washington vet's wife and I are not the only CRS sufferers. Indeed, from the mail and phone calls I received, CRS has reached epidemic proportions in this part of Oregon. People around here forget their children's names, their own phone numbers, and -- almost universally for those CRS victims over 40 -- their birth dates.

I was relieved to learn that not just people who work with animals suffer from CRS. I'd hate to think I got it from milk. But that can't be, because folks who wouldn't touch goat milk with a ten foot pole have some of the worst cases of the disease. One old geezer I know hasn't touched milk since he was weaned, and half the time he can't remember his wife's name. I suspected Alzheimer's, but his wife says he's been like that since they were married 35 years ago. One day she's Dorothy... the next, Diane.

My husband, on the other hand, drinks two quarts of goat milk a day and doesn't have the least sign of the disease. Maybe I should be drinking more. Milk, I mean.

Anyhow, it's a relief to know I'm not alone. Now when someone says "Hi" and I can't think of her name, I'm not embarrassed. I just say, "Sorry, my CRS is acting up again. What's your name?"

She pats me on the back and says kindly, "My name's Doris. But that's okay, Margie. I have the same problem."

In case you're wondering what the initials "CRS" stand for, I really can't remember. I think it's something like: "Can't Remember Manure".

KIDDING SEASON

KIDDING ADVICE

Those of us who have been through many kidding seasons tend to forget that new goatkeepers are terrified when their first doe kids. They don't know if she needs help, or if she's just groaning for effect. Beginners sometimes spend hours hanging over the pen of a doe who won't kid for another week. (So do old-timers -- if the doe is a permanent champion bred to a buck with a $100 service fee.) In the belief that beginners might appreciate some advice, here are a few tips from an experienced breeder for coping with kidding.

1. It's very important to be in attendance when a doe kids. Therefore, it's nice to know when she's getting ready. Check how loose the "cords" are on either side of the tail. When they can't be felt at all, the doe is either within six hours of kidding, or she's too fat. The only absolutely positive way to know when any doe is about to kid is to watch her rear end -- when a toe or nose appears, she's ready. If two noses appear, something's wrong. You have three choices: a) push one back; b) call a vet; c) run screaming into the night.

2. In order to be present at the birth, you either must make regular barn checks when a doe is nearing parturition (that's vet talk for birthing); sleep on a cot near the kidding pen; or install intercoms between house and barn. Each has advantages and drawbacks.

a. Regular barn checks are delightful when the weather is warm and sunny, and you're outside anyhow. Unfortunately, goats almost never kid on warm, sunny days. They prefer the middle of cold, sleety nights. Frequent hikes to the barn in the freezing rain and subsequent returns to bed with icy feet are very bad for dispositions -- especially your spouse's.

b. Sleeping on a cot near the kidding pen is the surest method of being there when it happens. If you don't sleep too soundly, you might even wake up in time to witness the glorious event. However, I only recommend this method for single goatkeepers. Spouses of goatkeepers tend to resent sleeping alone even more than they resent icy feet. I'm always worried that, if I leave my side of the bed vacant too long, I'll get replaced.

c. An intercom is the technique I prefer. It only takes three or four years of jumping out of bed every 15 minutes before you'll get accustomed to the strange noises emanating from your barn and learn to recognize the grunting sound of a doe in labor. If your husband or wife has not filed for divorce by that time, you're home free. (If your intercom suddenly stops making weird noises, your spouse turned it off without telling you. Turn it back on and offer to give him/her a massage to relax those muscles that are all tensed up from jumping every time a goat baas through the intercom into his/her ear.)

3. Keep calm. A doe will react to your mood. If you are pacing her pen, so will she. Only a few does have their kids on the run, so you both need to settle down and reflect on the wonders of nature. (I often wonder how nature can make the wind blow from sixteen directions at once, blowing snow through the cracks of the barn on top of me, no matter where I position myself.) Be aware that some does like to sit in your lap -- avoid this even though she's warmer than the snow. If her water breaks, you will have a very wet lap.

4. Have all your equipment ready -- iodine for dipping the umbilical cords, rough towels or burlap sacks for drying the babies, bottles and colostrum if you're not leaving the kids with their mothers, and the telephone number of the one friend who promised not to hang up on you no matter what hour you called to give her the glad news.

5. What if something goes wrong -- a doe strains for an hour without a little foot appearing? Scrub up and go in to see what's happening. If you can't figure it out and straighten it out in 15 minutes, call a vet. Nine times out of ten, a little help is all the doe needs -- uncurling a leg, pulling a head forward, or pushing an over-eager second kid back. A few such experiences and you'll gain self-confidence. After twenty, you'll no longer need a tranquilizer (or shot of whiskey) after each episode. You may then consider yourself an Experienced Goatkeeper.

You may have noticed that I never directly answered the critical questions of how to know -- for sure -- if your doe needs help, or how to know -- for sure -- when she is ready to kid. That's because I don't know those answers -- for sure. Each doe, each year, behaves differently. Each birth is unique. (Besides, experienced doesn't necessarily mean smart.)

The only thing predictable about kidding season on my farm is that I will cry when each kid takes his first tentative breath and when he first stands on his wobbly legs. I cry especially hard when he's the ninth "he" his momma has had with no daughters.

So here's my advice: be prepared; be calm; be there. But don't be surprised if you dash to the barn and find two licked-off kids snoozing beside their mother. It happens even to Experienced Goatkeepers.

FIRST FRESHENERS

Every year I ask myself the same question. Why do I freshen so many yearlings? In the fall, it made sense: keep them until they have udders. Yet some kids, I know, have zero chance of staying in my herd even if they develop beautiful udders. Like Coleen. Coleen was the loudest, most obnoxious kid I ever raised. Furthermore, I was fairly sure, by the feel of it, that her udder would be poorly attached. And her hocks rubbed together. So why did I keep her?

Because Coleen was named after a very nice person. I hated to give up on her. And she was the only doe kid from one of my bucks -- a buck I had high hopes for until his untimely death: he escaped and tried to breed the neighbor's bull. Surely his only daughter couldn't be bad, could she?

Yes. Worse.

In addition to being noisy, hocky and droopy-uddered, Coleen inherited her father's lack of common sense. She never figured out how to put her head into a keyhole feeder. On the milkstand, she rammed her nose back and forth against the narrow slot at the bottom, all the while screaming, instead of lifting her head and putting it through the wide hole at the top. Twice a day, I grabbed Coleen's head and lifted it through the hole. When she was done eating grain, I reversed the procedure. I once left the stupid doe on the stand for twenty minutes, thinking that, surely, in that time, she'd figure out how to escape. She didn't. She threw her body from side to side and hollered until she was hoarse -- but never lifted her head. Coleen was dumb. Real dumb. But then, so was I to keep her as long as I did.

Unlike Coleen, most kids have potential. So it's smart to freshen them before weeding them out. I think. Yet the last thing I need is a bunch of unproductive dry yearlings. So, as soon as doelings begin showing signs of heat, usually in September, I rush them to a buck.

Starting in September, I reason, gives me several months' leeway in case the kids don't get bred immediately. For some reason, it never occurs to me that does bred in September will freshen in February -- cold, icy, damp, dark February.

Yearlings are a bother no matter when they kid, but they bother me most in February. They call me out at all hours on sub-freezing nights -- loudly and persistently through the intercom that connects my bedroom with theirs. At least I've learned to wait for the screams. When I first acquired an intercom, I dashed out to the barn at the first groans and pawing sounds, then waited, shivering and pacing, for three hours until the action started.

Slow as yearlings are at birthing, most of them waste no time coming into the milk room. Charging past me, they run around the room five times before attempting a flying vault onto the milkstand. Often soaring clear off the opposite side.

After yearlings finally land on the milkstand, they turn into leaners, sit-downers, dancers and/or screamers. The biggest yearlings are always leaners. When I sit down to milk, they lean gratefully on me as though unable to hold their own weight a minute more. Gradually, they lean harder and harder, until I slump to the floor and they fall in the bucket.

Some yearlings start out in the bucket. The instant they feel my hands on their tender little udders they sit down -- trapping my wrists on top of the sharp edge of the pail, cutting off my circulation and nearly severing my wrists. Under these conditions, I can no longer squeeze teats, which I presume is what the does have in mind. A friend of mine once cured a habitual sit-downer by biting her in the flank. Although I've never tried that technique, I've been sorely tempted.

Dancers beat a tattoo on the milkstand -- or in the bucket. Every few steps they lift themselves into the air and come down somewhere else -- upsetting the milk pail on their way down. It is nearly impossible to protect a hard-won pail of milk from a dancer, because you never know where she's going to land next.

Screamers take a mouthful of grain and then scream, sending the grain cascading all over the room. Between bites, they turn their heads backwards 180 degrees and scream over their shoulders -- into my ear -- yelling for their babies, or friends, or maybe just to hear their own voices.

A screamer who is also a dancer is a nearly unbearable combination. As grain showers over me and into the pail, and my ears are assailed, all four feet beat a steady rhythm on the stand, or sometimes the bucket, as I struggle to keep my fingers from sliding off those microscopic teats. Millimeter by slow millimeter the bucket fills, while making frequent, rapid side trips out of the path of dancing feet. After milking four screamer/dancer yearlings, I have muscle cramps in both hands, a ringing in both ears, and a sorely frayed temper. Screamer/dancers must have perfect conformation and milk six gallons a day to stay in my herd.

However, whether a first freshener leans, sits down, screams or dances, I try hard to be patient, because I know they have good reason to be nervous. In the barn, they're learning the proper milking order from older does. The annual "wall-to-wall" counseling sessions have yearlings ricocheting off feeders, walls and water buckets. Quickly learning that a moving target is more difficult to hit than a stationary one, first fresheners flit from one side of the barn (or milk room) to the other, never standing still for more than five seconds.

Herd-matron Deedee guards the feeder on one side of the barn, while her twin sister, Delilah, keeps watch on the other.

"Here comes one of those brats now," baas Deedee. "WHAM."

"Nice shot," Delilah remarks. "Sending another your way... WHAM THUNK. Your serve."

After days, or sometimes weeks, yearlings realize that the milkstand is a refuge and that they don't need to run in place to avoid being broadsided. Eventually, their teats lengthen, their nerves...and mine...relax, and they become a comfortable part of the milking string.

By next September, I will have completely forgotten what it's like to deal with a bevy of first fresheners in the middle of winter. To haul bucket after bucket of hot water to newly-fresh mothers, who promptly poop in them. How can I think about snow and rain when the weather is hot and dry? What I do think about is fat, unbred yearlings eating up all the profits, or, more aptly, increasing the losses. And so I grab those doelings and shove them into the buck pen -- rushing kids into motherhood too early, yet again.

There really should be a law against first fresheners. I feel about them the way my husband feels about small children. He tried to get me to carry our babies for three years instead of nine months -- so they'd come out walking, talking and potty-trained. Someone should figure out a way to have does become instant second fresheners, ready-trained in milk parlor etiquette. Or else I need to figure out a way to remember that every kid I keep and breed will turn into an obnoxious yearling in five months. Alas, either solution appears equally unlikely.

MOTHERING
or
WAS IT
SOMETHING I ATE?

Baby goats usher in springtime on our farm. Some babies arrive with great fanfare and solicitous nickerings from their dams. Others are dropped on the floor and ignored. In my barn, the range of attitudes toward motherhood is extreme.

Deedee sets the standards for excellence. Thirteen years old with thirteen freshenings behind her, she has had lots of experience. I try to make the yearlings watch while Deedee gives birth, in hopes that they'll learn something.

"Girls, pay attention now. See what Deedee's doing?"

"Yuck," gags one yearling. "What's that gooey stuff she's eating off the floor?"

"Gross!" chorus the other pregnant, adolescent does.

Deedee is very tidy. She starts licking everything in sight long before the babies arrive. If I walk into her pen she gives me a thorough bath. Deedee cleans up every bit of birthing material that escapes before the baby. No predators would ever smell out her newborns. When baby moves into the birth canal, Deedee lies carefully down, strains, and reaches around to clean off her kid's head before the rest of its body enters the outside world. That's efficiency.

Deedee's twin sister, Delilah, has a different style. While Deedee usually has just two kids, Delilah specializes in multiple births -- from three to five. She solves the problem of tending to that many by spreading their births out over a long period of time. Like hours, or maybe days. By the time the last one is born, the first one's ready to be weaned.

Once a kid is on its way, Delilah stops mothering the last one and goes into her exercise routine. She jogs around the kidding pen, accelerating with every labor pain. With a final push, she drops the kid on its head and keeps moving until her circle brings her back around. Then she stops and cleans the new arrival. I try to catch the kids by sitting in the middle of her pen, but I get dizzy trying to keep an eye on her and generally miss the final expulsion.

I've often wondered what she'd do in an open field. Run a straight line dropping kids along the way? (With me chasing behind?) Delilah's kids are sturdy creatures who seem none the worse for having the breath knocked out of them before they've even taken one.

Both Deedee and Delilah are experts at helping their children find the milk spigots -- although they're such large spigots, a kid would have to be blind to miss them. The difficulty lies in getting the huge things into little, newborn mouths.

I often milk some colostrum into a bottle, both to deflate the teats a bit and to give the kids their first drink myself, which helps keep my momma-raised kids people-friendly. Deedee and Delilah do not approve and so work even harder to push their babies in the right direction. With her nose, Deedee can maneuver a kid into the correct position in no time. A little tickling in the rear quarters makes the front end start poking around for something to suck.

Not all my goats are as clever as Deedee and Delilah, nor that concerned with the welfare of their children. Total tries to make time in her busy schedule of stuffing her mouth with food to clean up her kids, but not to teach them to eat. "The faucets are there," she snaps. "If they're hungry enough, they'll find them."

Ellie takes good care of her kids once they're out, but she has a violent way of expelling them. Rather than gradual, sustained pushes, Ellie ejects her kids in forceful spurts -- sometimes propelling them five feet behind her -- into walls, water buckets, or whatever else is in the way. She acts more like a missile launcher than a mother.

The younger does haven't perfected their birthing techniques. In fact, they don't have the foggiest idea what's happening. They talk and lick and beg me to stay with them.

"Please, don't leave," cries a first freshener. "Something weird is happening to me."

"It's ok," I tell her. "You're just having a baby."

"Have *you* ever had a baby?" she questions.

"Yes, I've had two," I nod wisely.

"Does it hurt?"

"I don't want to talk about it."

"BAAAAAAAA!!"

"There, there," I soothe, holding her hoof until the kid is finally born. "Look! Here's your baby!" I announce triumphantly, laying the wet little thing by its mother's head.

She turns her face away and says: "That slimy thing? Forget it."

"Come on, now," I coax. "Clean it up and talk to it."

"You want it? *You* lick it. I'm exhausted."

After awhile, she relents and mothers her baby. Some yearlings even allow their kids to nurse. Others act like they're being goosed.

It's always interesting to see how yearlings react to their newborns. Deedee's offspring, whether by heredity or example, are good mothers. Total's are rather indifferent.

Some does are actually frightened by suddenly finding a wiggling, bleating, miniature goat in their pen.

"Good grief. Where did *that* come from?"

"From you," I tell them.

"You can't be serious. Was it something I ate?"

MUSICAL CHAIRS

Milkers are housed on the north side of my barn, dry yearlings in the southwest corner, yet-to-freshen does on the south side. Or that's the theory.

In fact, milkers sometimes overflow into the southwest pen, bumping dry yearlings into the pen of bred does. Weaned kids need a place, too, so they move into the outer pens, which are normally reserved for bucks. When the older weaned kids bully the younger ones (they always do), I separate them. I need more pens -- at least part of the year.

During the spring months, when does are freshening almost weekly, I constantly rearrange pen-mates, trying to keep everyone's quarters uncrowded. An impossible task, since I have too many goats for the size of my barn, as my dear husband frequently mentions.

This musical chairs in the goat barn is difficult for Johnny to cope with. He feeds hay in the evenings. Different types of hay go to different types of goats. Trouble is, he never knows which group is where.

"Johnny, didn't you feed the dry yearlings tonight? They're crying."

"I dunno; where are they?"

"In the outer pen next to Callisto."

"I thought that was an empty buck pen."

"It was yesterday. Today it's the dry yearling pen. And," I add, "don't forget the weaned kids in the northeast kidding pen. I didn't know where else to put them."

"How about the freezer?" Johnny can be terribly snide.

When the sun is shining, the goats spend most of their time out in the pastures. However, we need more crossfencing to keep the various groups separate. Johnny turns pale and shaky when I talk about more fences.

"You have goats in six different pastures now. How many more do you need?"

"About five. I have four bucks. They can live together part of the year, but when they each have their own little herd of does to breed, they need separate pastures. That's four. Then I have milkers, dry does (I don't want them eating the milkers' alfalfa), weaned kids, and pregnant does. That's four more, or eight all together and I only have six fields."

"But you said five more, not two more."

"Well, I'm sure they'll be used. I always fill up every space I have."

"That," mutters Johnny, "is what I'm afraid of."

After the rains begin in the fall, I need less pasture space, but more inside pen space. The goats won't leave the barn in bad weather, but they'd like more room. So they try to convince their pen-mates to leave. The older does push the yearlings outside, big kids push smaller kids out, and so on.

"We need another barn," I tell Johnny.

"You have finally gone over the edge, haven't you?" responds Johnny.

"What do you mean?"

"If you think I would even consider building another barn for you to fill with more goats, you're completely crazy."

"I don't want more goats," I explain, "just more places to put the ones I have."

"Okay. We'll buy another freezer."

"Johnny, listen. Even with half as many goats as I have now, I'd need another barn. For the bucks."

"If you had half as many bucks, you'd only need a two-stall barn. We have one of those in the far northwest pasture."

"That's the horses' lean-to, and it's a quarter mile away," I protest.

"Yeah," he agrees. "A good distance for bucks."

I can tell this discussion is going nowhere, so I start shuffling goats again, trying to find combinations that eat the same feed and get along together.

"What are these goats doing in the aisle?" asks Johnny, as he trips over a kid.

"I didn't have any other place to put them. Too bad we don't have another barn, huh?"

"Hmmph. Too bad you don't have another hobby. Like stamp collecting. It takes less room."

But I don't collect stamps; I collect goats, and goats take up room -- sometimes one room, sometimes another.

"I'll bet if I moved goats into the bedroom, you'd build me another barn," I threaten.

"You're right. And I'd move *you* into it... Doesn't that good-looking divorcee down the road collect stamps?"

AUCTION DAY

I don't sell goats at the auction. I'm afraid they'll be mistreated by the buyer. My excess goats are either turned into sausage or kept until I find a prospective owner who meets my rigorous specifications.

That is, until one fateful spring. That spring, Johnny was too busy to butcher goats, and I don't trust anyone else to do it humanely. Buyers were few and far between. Does were starting to kid, and I was starting to realize that my barn has limits. When a goat can't turn around without bumping into another goat, the limits have been reached.

So I started thinking about the auction. Most of my friends routinely sell their goats there, with no qualms.

"Why do you think people who buy at an auction are any worse than those who buy at your farm?" another goat breeder asked me. "They're just looking for bargains."

Of course my friend is right. Most people, whether they buy from the farm or from an auction, like animals and don't mistreat them. Or so I told myself over and over. After all, I've been known to buy animals at auctions, and I'm nice.

For weeks, I worked at convincing myself. Finally, I told several friends that I was taking goats to the auction *next week*. If I didn't go, I'd be a liar, so I'd have to follow through. Or so I reasoned.

Next week came and I plodded slowly through chores. I milked out the does I intended to take. So what if they would sell better with full udders? I didn't want them bouncing painfully around in the back of somebody's open pickup. Open pickup? Oh, no! How could I sell my pampered goats to an unknown person who just might haul them in an open pickup? In the rain? However, it wasn't raining on auction day. It was sunny and quite warm, considering we'd had frost the night before.

I stalled until it was almost too late to go. "Linda," I told myself, "You can't chicken out now. Do you want to be milking 40 goats in another month? Do you want to stay married?" The answers were obvious. I started flying around.

My husband, seeming *very* anxious to accommodate me, had left the van for me to use. I dashed to the shop, climbed behind the wheel, and turned on the key. The first two grinds on the starter almost brought the engine to life. The third time, there was nothing but silence. Not even a click. I tried again and again. Wiggled wires. Jiggled the gear shift lever. Nothing.

Maybe I wasn't destined to go to the auction, I thought hopefully.

No! I'd made up my mind. No phony excuses. I'd just have to take the little Datsun station wagon. All five goats would fit. After all, two were babies. I charged upstairs to get the old, stiff tarp we use to protect the back of the wagon. Throwing it in the back, I began to spread it out. As I opened the last fold, approximately five million flies that had been peacefully hibernating started to slowly awaken.

AARGH!

I grabbed the tarp, pulled it out and shook it. Flies by the hundreds rose groggily up, or tumbled to the ground. A few hundred more were still in the wagon, crawling about in the warmth of the car -- or were already airborne. Just what I needed: a few thousand flies buzzing around my face while I drove. Maybe the auction wasn't such a good idea.

No! I wouldn't let flies stop me. I put the tarp back in and looked around for a piece of plywood that would fit behind the front seat, to keep the older does from jumping into my lap. I found one upstairs (everything in my husband's shop is upstairs except the cars); wrestled it downstairs, banging it against my shins with every step; and wedged it behind the seat. Then I drove to the barn. The two kids, wethered and disbudded, were easy to load. I put them on the floor of the front seat. The milkers and dry two-year-old would have to share the back.

The morning sun had already turned the frosty ground to mud, and the three does were reluctant to be led out of their dry quarters. By alternately pleading and dragging, I succeeded in getting them to the car. Then the fun began.

Our station wagon is a hatchback. I lifted up the rear door, stuffed a goat in, and slammed the door down quickly -- on my arm. Muttering in pain, I grabbed another goat, opened the hatch, holding the first goat at bay with my injured arm while I attempted to stuff the other one inside. With one desperate thrust, I pushed both goat bodies in, as the car door came crashing down -- on the small of my back. With tears streaming out of my eyes, I wondered if taking goats to the auction was worth permanent bodily injury.

But I'd come this far, and I wouldn't give up. Through the mists of pain, my brain realized that if I tied each goat as I loaded her, she couldn't jump back out. But I was out of time. The auction would start without me if I didn't leave instantly. In desperation, I grabbed the last goat and threw her in the car on top of the other two. So much for gentle and careful handling. I slammed the door -- for once without including part of my anatomy; wiped the mud and manure off my hands; jumped in the driver's seat, which was now, of course, occupied by two wether kids; and roared off.

The flies loved the smell of my sweat, mud and manure. They swarmed over me. The does screamed their displeasure. I drove faster. I had no choice: the kids had settled down on top of the accelerator.

When I arrived at the fairgrounds, I followed big cattle trucks to the unloading docks, feeling foolish in my little green station wagon. I felt even more foolish when it was my turn at the docks and a big, burly man with a whip told me I was in the wrong line. "Goats and sheep are unloaded at the side, lady."

I slunk out of that line and drove to the back of another. This line had smaller pickups, most of which, I noticed in some relief, sported canopies. Nearly every goat person in the county was at the auction that day... and they all came up to me as I waited in line. "What are you doing here, Linda? I thought you never sold goats at the auction. Are these that bad? Hah, hah."

If I weren't stubborn, and too tired to turn the steering wheel hard enough to pull out of line, I would have driven back home. But at last it was my turn. I opened the hatch... and the goats refused to come out. They didn't like the look or sound of things. And I didn't blame them. Calves bawled, cows mooed, pigs squealed, sheep bleated, goats baaed and people hollered. The only sound lacking was the buzzing of flies, but that was loud enough inside the car.

I dragged the unwilling goats out and watched anxiously as the attendant smeared glue on numbered stickers and slapped them on my sleek and unsuspecting goats. Then I left. I couldn't bear to see who bid on them. I'd probably have bought them back myself.

A few days later, the check arrived. The goats had brought good money, much more than they were worth as meat. Maybe I'll take goats to the auction more often, I thought... After my arm, shins, and back heal and my memory fades.

Then again, what's wrong with milking 40 goats?

CUTTING DOWN

Somewhere my herd reduction plans have gone wrong. One year I really did sell all but three of my older does. "So why," asked my cynical husband the next spring, "do you have thirteen does fresh already with six more still in waiting?"

It's like this: I hate to sell kids before I see their udders. I wouldn't mind selling someone a national champion, but I'd hate to sell him a dud. Well, anyway, that's the excuse I gave Johnny for keeping twelve dry yearlings, then freshening them as two-year-olds.

"Why didn't you go ahead and freshen them last year and then *sell* most of them?" queried my relentless spouse.

"I didn't want to milk that many goats!" (Seems perfectly obvious to me; why not to him?)

"But you *are* milking that many this year -- and more -- all last year's kids, too!"

"No, I'm not. I'm leaving the kids with their mothers."

"Oh, wonderful. That should really cut down on the goat population in the barn." (Sometimes Johnny can be very sarcastic.)

I must confess, there *are* a lot of goats in our barn, big ones and little ones... and more little ones -- under mangers, under other goats, underfoot.

One night Johnny was helping feed hay while I milked. (Yes, milked. All the does give more milk than their kids can drink and besides, I want to keep production up). I heard a loud THUD, clatter of buckets, and the sound of many hooves hurriedly scattering, intermixed with epithets from my partner.

"What happened?!" I asked as I dashed to the scene of the accident.

He looked up at me from his damp, ungainly position on the barn floor, sprawled among water buckets and goat berries, and said casually, although somewhat unpleasantly, "Oh, I was just trying to wade through fifty baby goats without stepping on or tripping over them, that's all."

"Now, Johnny, there are only fourteen babies in this pen."

"Fourteen kids running back and forth under me at least four times each makes fifty-six. I underestimated."

"I'm sorry." What else could I say?

Perhaps what I lack is commitment. If I really, deep down inside, wanted to cut my herd down to four or five goats, as I have professed in wild moments, I'd do it. But even while I'm saying that I need more time for other activities, or just for LESS activity, visions of show strings dance in my head. It's pretty hard to have a show string with only four goats in the barn, two of which are great-great-grandmothers, a bit worse for wear but part of the family.

However, after lifting the twelfth untrained first freshener onto the milking platform, cutting down seems like a very good plan indeed. It's just this sort of vacillation that has kept my herd around thirty (not counting babies, of course) for several years.

Once Johnny came home and said, "I think I sold three goats for you."

My heart stopped. I squeaked in horror, "Which three?"

"Oh, I just told them we had any kind of goat they wanted. They're coming by tomorrow afternoon."

And they did. A very sweet elderly couple looking for three pygmy goats. I don't have pygmies, so I directed them elsewhere. That was a close call.

When I do sell goats, it's almost always with first buy-back rights. Since many goat folk sell out after a few years and go back to spending time with their families, I'm not infrequently given an opportunity to buy back one of my sales. After one doe came back three times, Johnny wanted to know what was wrong with her.

"Nothing," I replied defensively. "It's just that her owners keep going out of the goat business."

"Keep her," he said. "Maybe she'll bring US that kind of luck."

To Johnny's dismay, she brought us four doe kids instead. I tried to appease him by naming one kid, "That Kind of Luck".

He wasn't amused.

MEDICATING

My goats are pretty healthy, but no one seeing my arsenal of syringes and needles would believe that.

"Good grief, Linda," said a non-goat friend, juggling Tetanus anti-toxin, Bo-Se bottles, and other assorted paraphernalia, as she followed me to the barn. "Are all your goats sick?"

"Oh, no," I explained. "I'm just giving them routine inoculations. You know, like the DPT shots your kids get."

"Sure glad I don't have thirty kids," she sighed.

At times, I wish I had fewer kids, too. Like when I'm giving shots. I'm always afraid I'll stab myself instead of the goat -- and sometimes I do.

I hate giving pills, too. But now that I've switched from boluses to paste wormers, life is a little easier. In the old days, more medicine landed on the barn floor than in goat stomachs. Some of my goats could hold boluses under their tongues for hours. They waited until I went to the house before spitting out and tromping on the vile tasting things.

Paste wormers are much easier to use -- except when I forget to secure the plunger. Then, the plunger goes all the way in and my 125 pound doe gets a 1500 pound dose. I have some of the best wormed goats in the country.

The sheer number of routine operations my goats need wears me down -- shots, hoof trimming, deworming, udder clipping, tattooing, disbudding. When illness strikes, I get hysterical.

One year, pneumonia hit. This was back in the days before I gave up on extraordinary life-saving measures and let natural selection take over. I came tearfully into the house after finding the first kid crying in pain and breathing hard. "All the babies are going to die. I just know they are," I sobbed to my husband. "I can't stand treating all these goats -- I hate giving shots."

"How many are sick?" he asked.

"One."

But I always imagined the worst. Each day I fearfully checked each goat, and was amazed that they were all still breathing.

Pneumonia has quit visiting my farm ever since I quit treating kids and let the weak ones die and the strong ones recover on their own. But I still panic when a milker goes off feed. Quick! Dose her with corn syrup! Or baking soda! See if she'll eat chocolate chip cookies! I clamp my ear to her side, listening anxiously for rumen gurglings. No sound? Grab another goat's cud and stuff it down the sick one's throat.

Cud-grabbing takes finesse... or *something* that I don't have. Nonchalantly, I stand petting a doe, watching her and all the others carefully -- waiting for a wad to move up a throat and into a mouth. The minute a goat starts chewing her cud, I grab her lower jaw and reach my fingers in for a piece of that rumen-stimulating glop -- and lose a finger. By the third attempt, every goat on the place, deciding that I'm certifiably crazy, is cowering in the corner, watching me in wild-eyed wonder.

Once in awhile, I succeed. The recipient goat is about as eager to swallow the life-saving hunk of foul-smelling, regurgitated hay as the donor was to give it. If, however, I do manage to cram a piece of cud down a sick doe, she usually starts eating again. Maybe just so I'll leave her alone.

If a cud or corn syrup or cookies don't work, I'm in trouble. I hate calling vets. They always ask embarrassing questions -- like, "What's her temperature?" I don't like to take temperatures. My goats don't care for it either.

And, "What have you done for her so far?" Veterinarians are never impressed when I answer, "I baked her a batch of chocolate chip cookies." They always want me to "bring her in". Vets don't understand how difficult it is to load a goat who's not interested in cookies. I sit in the back of the truck, eating chocolate chippers, hoping she'll join me. If she hasn't jumped in by the time the cookies are gone, I figure she's too sick to travel. Or anyway I am after all those cookies.

Fortunately, my goats are rarely that sick -- maybe because they hate medications as much as I do.

WEIRD VETS

In spite of my belief in letting the fittest goats survive and the others become bologna, I still use a veterinarian at times. My long-time vet now has a second vet working with him, who, for some reason, is the one I'm always assigned to. He is a very strange man. Veterinarians are all strange. They get excited over the oddest things. When I had my first ever case of milk fever, my vet had never seen a goat with milk fever, either.

"Yes, sir, looks like a classic case. How about that! See? Her eyes are dilated and don't contract with light. Well, what do you know. My professor told me goats were resistant to milk fever."

My vet acted thrilled to have proven his prof wrong. I just wanted him to save my goat. Ilsa had seemed fine when she freshened with three big kids. I'd turned her out with the herd the next day -- sooner than usual because her kids were so big and sturdy and I needed her kidding pen for another about-to-pop doe.

I worked in the barn most of the day, and didn't think it odd that Ilsa was out in the pasture grazing, while her mother stayed by the barn babysitting everybody else's kids. Lots of grandmas get stuck with that job. I didn't even spark when Ilsa came in later and would have nothing to do with her babies. I thought she was just being cantankerous, so I locked her in a pen and made her let them eat. When I milked that night, Ilsa was lying down and didn't want to get up. I thought she just didn't want three babies poking at her. Not that I blamed her, but they needed to eat, so I got her to her feet. She staggered forward and collapsed.

Panic stricken, I ran for the house and telephone. "Sounds like milk fever," the vet said. "Can you load her up and bring her in?" Johnny and one of our teenaged sons were home so I said yes. Four-year-old Ilsa weighs a ton, I've now decided. Johnny says she's closer to 175 pounds. Whatever, the three of us had all we could do to carry her to the van.

I sat in the back with Ilsa, cradling her head and muttering profuse apologies for not realizing she was in trouble, while Johnny drove the thirty twisty mountain miles to the vet's office. I get car sick very easily, and by the time we reached the vet's, I was feeling as bad as Ilsa.

The vet, however, was in a fine mood. "I can't be sure without tests, but there's no time for those, and this acts like milk fever in cows. She's just a little Jersey, isn't she? Heh, heh."

Nauseous and worried, I found it hard to share his cheerfulness. The vet hooked up the IV and started running a calcium mix into Ilsa's veins. While watching her respiration rate and heartbeat, he chattered about this and that.

Suddenly, Ilsa belched -- a great, rolling belch that went on and on.

"Hooray!" shouted the vet. "Hear that?! That's wonderful." Ilsa, as though warming to the praise, belched again and again. By now the vet was practically leaping up and down with joy and I began to think we'd taken our goat to a lunatic.

Seeing the look on my face, he laughed. "Vets are weird people. We love hearing animals with milk fever belch. It means their muscles are working again. When the calcium drains from their system, they can't urinate, defecate, or belch. To us vets, a belch is beautiful music."

About then, Ilsa let out another chorus of sound. This time, it sounded good to me, too.

After a few minutes, the vet encouraged Ilsa to stand, which she did, and promptly pooped on my shoe. "Great!" he exclaimed. Then she peed, and I jerked my foot back. The vet hollered "All right!" and stuck a little pill under the stream of urine. "Look here! She's not ketotic anymore! See? It didn't turn purple."

I've seen people less excited over sitting down to a sirloin steak dinner than this guy was to seeing a pill that didn't change color when he drenched it in urine.

Ilsa was soon fine. I'm not so sure about that vet.

But he's really no different from his colleague, who tried years ago to teach me how to identify internal parasites. That vet had slides of lots of parasites, a chart and names. I looked through his fancy microscope and saw -- little round things.

"Look here!" he beamed. "Liver fluke eggs!"

I looked and saw -- little round things, that looked just like all the other little round things.

"Isn't this a great microscope?!" he enthused.

"Yeah, great," I agreed. With it, you could see all the little round things you'd ever want to see. How you'd tell them apart I don't know.

But, in an effort to check the efficiency of my worming treatments, I bought a flotation kit and a book called "Veterinary Clinical Parasitology." In that book, I learned the truth.

"Because of the similarity in egg morphology of a number of the gastrointestinal nematodes of cattle, sheep, and goats in North America it is difficult to identify the worm by a fecal examination." Boy, I'll say. In even smaller letters at the bottom of the page: "Note: Cattle, sheep, and goats in North America harbor 27 species of gastrointestinal nematodes, the eggs of which are similar in morphology."

Yeah. They're all little round things that look identical. Maybe with enough experience I could learn to tell them apart, but I doubt I'd ever get as excited about finding a liver fluke as my vet, so I take my fecal samples to him. It's fun to watch him hop about. "Oh, boy! Lookee here! A coccidium oocyst!"

Personally, I'd prefer a steak dinner.

TIPS ON
LOADING GOATS

Goats do a lot of traveling -- to shows, auctions, new homes, the vet. Before a move, goat owners would be well advised to give their animals shipping fever shots -- and themselves tranquilizers. Anyone who has ever traveled in a car full of screaming Nubian kids understands why. If you haven't, just imagine the sound of a supersonic jet taking off -- inside your car.

Loading goats *should* be a whole lot easier than loading, say, elephants, just because goats are smaller. However, that theory has pitfalls. No one would ever try to stuff an elephant into the back seat of a Volkswagen; an elephant is obviously too big. A goat isn't. However, after being pushed unwillingly someplace, a goat is unlikely to stay put. Five miles down the road, all backseat goats become frontseat goats -- on the driver's lap and the gas pedal. Try explaining to a policeman that you were speeding and driving erratically because you had a goat on your lap. This is somewhat easier to do if the goat is still on your lap -- eating the ticket.

A pickup truck with an enclosed canopy is the favored rig for hauling goats. Favored by people, but not necessarily by goats. Goats would prefer not to travel at all. Some of my goats, I admit, are wonderfully cooperative about jumping into trucks. But, having seen the view from inside, they jump right back out. Keeping the first one in while the second is loaded requires more than one person. Twenty-three would be ideal.

Unfortunately, when I load my animals, I'm usually alone, or else have only one helper -- my husband. Johnny has very little patience with goats, or with me. He expects a doe to follow politely at his side when he grabs her collar. She doesn't. She breaks and runs, ripping his fingers out of their sockets.

Being strong, Johnny is good at lifting stubborn does into our vehicle. That leaves me to keep five goats at bay, while he dumps another one in. Often I fail. That's when my spouse loses patience with me. Johnny does not like lifting the same goat ten times. We usually "have words" before the van is loaded.

To prevent domestic turmoil, we now tie the goats once they're in the van. Of course, they immediately strangle themselves, get wrapped around and under each other until one of them smothers, or rear back and break the rope -- or their necks.

When just a couple of goats are going somewhere, I use my little station wagon. Everyone knows goats don't mess in a car unless they absolutely have to. Unless I'm meeting my in-laws at the airport later the same day with no time to clean the rig.

"Let's just put the suitcases in the back on top of this blanket," I suggest cheerfully.

"What are those lumps under the blanket?" my father-in-law asks suspiciously.

"Oh, heh heh. Just a little straw and stuff."

After a few miles in a warm car, the "straw and stuff" has us all leaning out the open windows, gasping for air.

My car, however, has never been able to compete in aroma with the car that transported a full-grown buck -- during breeding season -- from Oregon to California. An airline pilot bought the buck from an Oregon breeder, flew up from Los Angeles on his regular flight, then rented a car for the drive back. He took the rear seat out of the rental, lined the cavity with plastic, and loaded the 400 pound buck. One thousand miles with a buck in the back seat -- during breeding season. For the driver's sake, I hope he never passed any cars with does in them. A warm buck is bad enough; an excited one would be unbearable. I've often wondered if the buck buyer had nerve enough to return that rental car, or if he just burned it and paid the bill.

One compensation to traveling with goats is watching the surprised expressions of passers-by. Nubian breeders, however, try to avoid towns with stop signs. Every time the rig stops, the goats call for help. Not even honking horns can drown out a half dozen hollering Nubians. I'm always afraid some do-gooder will call the humane society and turn me in -- the hysterical sounding screams (some of them mine), suggest a mobile torture chamber.

A friend totes her goats about in the trunk of her car. The trunk space holds plenty of air because it's only marginally separated from the car's interior. The only reason no one has ever turned *her* in is because she raises quiet Saanens instead of noisy Nubians. I still marvel that she's able to close the trunk lid without beheading a goat or severing her own hand.

Unloading goats is a real pleasure. Just open the door (or trunk lid), and get out of the way. The happy critters jump down and run -- straight to the nearest fruit tree or rose bush. If they're at a fair, they head for the nearest grain sack, usually owned by some goat-hating cattleman. They knock over the bag (and sometimes the cattleman), then tromp and poop on the grain.

My advice to beginning goat owners who are thinking of going somewhere with their goats is: don't. Take their photos with you and leave the goats at home.

SPRING CLEANING

Every spring the day arrives when I must either clean the barn or breed shorter goats. The winter manure and straw pack builds up until the goats walk around on their knees -- or stand up and bonk their heads on the ceiling.

One year, spring came later than usual, and so did spring cleaning. I wasn't procrastinating; I just wanted the weather to warm before I took away the hot compost. Also, I needed a day when the three men of the household would be home -- and I wouldn't. (They work so much faster than I do, it seems a shame to get in their way.)

By the time Cleaning Day arrived, spring was a distant memory and the manure pack was nearly hot enough to roast marshmallows. Before I was done milking, my husband arrived at the barn, with pitchfork. Since Johnny will not work with curious critters bothering him, he tried to move all the goats into an adjacent pen. That's when the trouble began.

For some reason, as soon as my husband tries to shoo a goat into a different pen, that goat decides her life depends on not going. She sidesteps, dodges, and keeps safely out of his reach. I know it's time to intervene when my husband's roar rattles the milkhouse windows.

"Johnny, wait!" I pleaded as he aimed a kick at a retreating goat. "I'll move the girls. You man the gate."

By now, the goats were having a wonderful time, with no intention of giving up the game. Instead of coming docilely up to me as usual, does and kids frolicked just out of reach, playing keep away.

"Try to catch me. Hah, hah. You missed."

My patience was wearing thin and Johnny's was exploding when the goats suddenly stopped and allowed me to lead them, one at a time, to the gate.

Then our two sons showed up. Normally, they stay as far from the barn and chores as possible, but I guess chasing goats looked like fun.

"Here, Mom, let's just herd them through. It'll be faster.

"Whoop! Whoop! Giddup goats!" shouted my teenage helpers as they waved their arms and charged the animals.

Pandemonium broke loose again. My husband groaned. I screamed at our sons, while goat kids ricocheted off walls and feeders.

"I caught one!" yelled a triumphant child. I looked just as a 200 pound doe pulled my eldest son off his feet and dragged him across the barnyard.

Seconds before my husband shot all the goats, and I shot my sons, the goats decided they'd rather be in the other pen anyway and trotted happily through the gate. A few kids were loathe to give up this entertaining game, but, finally, even they were cornered and captured.

Barn cleaning was ready to begin, an hour late, with all participants hot and tired. I finished chores and disappeared. (I forget what I had to leave to do, but I'm sure it was important.)

That night when I returned, the barn was clean, the goats were back in their own pen, and all but the last load of manure was spread on the fields. That load could wait until the weather cooled enough for us to start a fire in the wood stove, generating more ashes to add to the manure. (We use wood ashes to "lime" our fields.) Such time came quickly, because as soon as the warm manure pack was gone, of course, another cold, rainy spell arrived.

I didn't realize my husband had dumped the ashes from the morning's fire on top of the manure load until I came home that afternoon to see smoke billowing up from behind the barn.

"Something's on fire!" I yelled and ran for the barn. Flames were leaping out of the manure spreader.

"Oops," said my husband, as he appeared on the scene. "I thought the ashes were cool enough. Guess they weren't, huh?"

While smoke curled threateningly through the barn, I ran for a hose. Johnny, on the other hand, calmly hitched up the tractor and spread the smoking manure over the soggy pasture.

"What's dad doing?" asked one of our sons, as he sauntered out of the house.

"Spreading hot ashes on the field," I replied.

Kevin took a long look at the smoke plumes wafting up from the field behind the manure spreader and at the curious goats following, who started dancing as their tender toes met flaming compost.

"Pretty drastic cure for foot rot, isn't it?"

ABOUT THE AUTHOR

Animals have been Linda's lifelong love. She graduated from the University of Illinois with a BS degree in Zoology. In 1969, she and her unsuspecting husband Johnny bought their first goats. Their two sons, Kevin and Steve, were raised on goat's milk, which is why, according to Linda, they are so healthy and so brilliant. Linda says you can tell how smart her kids are because they are both going to college to be something, anything, other than goat farmers.

Besides tending Nubians on their 45 acre farm near Grand Ronde, Oregon, Linda writes a weekly humor column for an Oregon newspaper, the Sheridan Sun. *She also writes* The Kidding Pen, *a monthly column in* United Caprine News, *from which the stories in this book were adapted. Linda's humorous writings have appeared in numerous other regional and national publications.*

ABOUT THE ARTIST

Commercial artist Barbara Millikan says she has "been getting in trouble for cartooning since elementary school", when she was caught drawing caricatures of her teachers. Barbara owned her own graphics business in Berkeley, California, for six years before moving to Oregon. She also drew comic books, cartoon strips, and political cartoons for San Francisco Bay area publications.

Now when Barbara isn't drawing, she's writing for the Salem Statesman-Journal *newspaper. She and her husband Mark, four-year-old daughter Lynn, two dogs and one cat -- but no goats -- live on a 55 acre farm near Sheridan, Oregon. They did keep two brush goats, Brahms and Mozart, for a short time... until they escaped and raided the garden. Mozart's hide still hangs on the wall of their back porch.*